The Last Words
of the Resurrected Christ

The Last Words of the Resurrected Christ

Richard O. Singleton

Saint Mary's Press
Christian Brothers Publications
Winona, Minnesota

To Sharron, my companion along the Way,
and to our offspring, Andrea and Matthew.
Praise be to the resurrected Lord.

 Genuine recycled paper with 10% post-consumer waste.
Printed with soy-based ink.

The publishing team included Carl Koch, development editor; Jacqueline M.
Captain, manuscript editor; Barbara Bartelson, typesetter; Maurine R. Twait,
art director; Nicholas Markell, Markell Studios, illustrator; Shirley Kelter,
calligrapher; cover art courtesy of Saint Isaac of Syria Skete; pre-press, printing, and binding by the graphics division of Saint Mary's Press.

The acknowledgments continue on page 91.

Printed in the United States of America

Printing: 9 8 7 6 5 4 3 2 1

Year: 2005 04 03 02 01 00 99 98 97

ISBN 0-88489-368-5

Contents

Introduction

But in fact Christ has been raised from the dead, the first fruits of those who have died. For since death came through a human being, the resurrection of the dead has also come through a human being; for as all die in Adam, so all will be made alive in Christ. (1 Corinthians 15:20–22)

Living the Resurrected Life

In Christ, all will be made alive! In the West we tend to be Christians of the cross. Lent as a season of preparation for Easter did not exist until the fifth century. Pope Gregory the Great felt there needed to be more piety in the church, so he created Lent. Before this reformation, Easter was the focus in liturgy, theology, and piety.

After this reform, a gradual and subtle change in the primary theology of the church took place. The focus shifted from the enablement of disciples through the power of God manifested through the Resurrection: being "made alive" through the gift of resurrection faith. With the establishment of Lent, the church became an organized mechanism for the remission of sin and reconciliation to God. Focusing on the Resurrection emphasized discipleship for mission. Focusing on Lent led to dependency on ecclesial power. The former emphasizes the empowerment of a liberating and healing people. The latter reflects ecclesiasticism, a church of sheep.

What Were the Last Words of Christ?

Ask yourself: What were the last words of Jesus Christ? What words come into your mind when this question is asked? I have given this simple quiz to many people.

In popular piety when we think of the last words of Jesus, we usually think of the final words of Jesus on the cross: "'Father, forgive them; for they do not know what they are doing'" (Luke 23:34), or "'Father, into your hands I commend my spirit'" (Luke 23:46), or "'It is finished'" (John 19:30). Indeed these are the final words of the earthly Jesus as recorded in the Scriptures. Much has been made of them, such as the traditional musical setting by Marcel Dupré, *The Seven Last Words*. Popular Anglican piety observes the ritual three hours on Good Friday, from noon until three, by having the faithful mortify the flesh, especially their knees and posteriors, while listening to repeated sermons on Jesus' seven last words.

On the other hand, when do you remember spending three hours in church listening to ten meditations on the last words of the resurrected Christ? Most likely, I think the answer is never. The final words—the final teaching and instruction of the resurrected Christ—are not part of popular piety.

In my experience, 95 percent of all people, including trained clergy, fail the simple test with which I opened this chapter. Very few say that the last words of Christ were, "'And remember, I am with you always, to the end of the age'" (Matthew 28:20) or any of the other words of the resurrected Jesus. This book is intended to change this. I hope these meditations on the last words of the resurrected Christ will be an antidote for this lack of positive resurrection theology and missionary focus in the western church.

On Easter Sunday we pull out the stops for one day, or more realistically yet, maybe for one and a half hours. Large numbers of the faithful attend church to view the mystical rites associated with the vernal equinox, then disappear from the pews, sometimes until Christmas. Meanwhile the Easter season in which the great stories of Easter that center on God's empowerment of those who experience the Resurrection are missed.

Easter is a season with as many Sundays as Lent but, in the western church, it is a season that is seldom observed with the same intensity as Lent. The faithful sense something special about Easter, otherwise they would not be in the pews in such astounding numbers on Easter Sunday. But they seldom stay around long enough to seriously examine the matter. Even among the clergy, who ought to know better, there is the feeling that after Easter Sunday the church season is mostly over. Indeed the Sunday immediately following Easter Sunday has become affectionately known as Low Sunday, because church attendance sharply declines. After all most of us went for the big day. Many of the clergy even take off the week after Easter Sunday.

What Happens to Easter?

So what happens to Easter and the Easter season with its focus on the empowerment that is received through the Resurrection of the Christ and the teaching of the resurrected Christ? It gets lost. An effective theology of Easter and the Easter experience of hope seems to have vanished. Most of us find the Resurrection a neglected conundrum. Few of us have consciously experienced the power of the resurrected Christ in our personal life.

Perhaps the popular mindset about the Resurrection is best seen in how Hollywood attempts to depict the final days of Christ. His time with us ends with some music and a mighty burst of light that is supposed to symbolize the Resurrection. Little attention is paid to the period after the Resurrection with its ensuing appearances, teaching, and the empowerment of the disciples. Many Hollywood depictions end with the Crucifixion or a brief melodramatic Resurrection. The movie *The Gospel of Matthew* glides over the Resurrection; *Jesus Christ Superstar* has a vague musical rendering; *The Last Temptation of Christ* ends with a fantasy on the cross.

The resurrected Jesus clearly poses problems for media depiction, as well as for theologians. The recent movie *Ghost* makes an excellent attempt to formulate in a visual way notions of an afterlife and the effects of such a spirit world on our world. One can only wonder how a similar treatment of the Resurrection of Jesus and his subsequent appearances would turn out.

The present state of historical-critical interpretation of the Christian Testament has reached the ultimate absurdity concerning the Resurrection. Some theologians have essentially reduced the Gospel message to what is acceptable only according to modern scientific presuppositions, historical methodology, or pop psychology. So not only did Jesus not rise from the dead, but he is cast as a new age mystical teacher or as an itinerant religious radical revolutionary without the use of guns or physical violence.

But Christ Is Risen

The Christian Testament, the Gospels and the Epistles, gives clear testimony to Jesus' Resurrection. If Jesus did not rise from the dead, there would be no victory over death and sin. Paul states the issue succinctly: "If Christ has not been raised, then our proclamation has been in vain and your faith has been in vain. . . . If Christ has not been raised, your faith is futile" (1 Corinthians 15:14–17). In fact, Jesus' Resurrection planted the seeds of a total spiritual revolution that has continued for two millennia: no bodily Resurrection, no revolution!

Paul adds: "In fact Christ has been raised from the dead. . . . So all will be made alive in Christ" (1 Corinthians 15:20–22). Put simply: no Resurrection, no life. We are still in bondage to sin and death. The Resurrection of Christ equals life, death conquered, sin overcome.

We Do Experience Christ Resurrected

The main thesis of this book is that we still experience the resurrected Jesus Christ today. The Resurrection stories of the Gospels hold the key to what is real and what is important for living and understanding the meaning of life.

In the Gospel of John, Jesus says to Nicodemus, "'Very truly, I tell you, no one can see the kingdom of God without being born from above'" (3:3). He also says, "'What is born of the flesh is flesh, and what is born of the Spirit is spirit'" (3:6). In order to encounter the resurrected Christ, we need to embrace a mystery that stretches our usual ways of knowing.

The Resurrection stories of the Gospels challenge our sensate way of looking at reality. They tell us that reality is much larger than we think it is or than we can even normally perceive. We must be challenged by the word of God and by the words of the resurrected Jesus to a new experience of our existence. Thus we meditate and invite the Spirit to lead our spirit into new adventures beyond our normal horizon of perception and understanding. The Spirit leads us into life eternal.

The last words of the Risen Christ offer a pattern for living the resurrected life, the new life, the life empowered by God. They are words of eternal life to all who hear them, meditate upon them, receive them into their heart and mind, and act on them.

Meeting God Imaginatively Through the Scriptures

The Scriptures are sacrament, that is, they are the spiritual world embodied in physical words and stories. As sacrament, the Scriptures are a vehicle through which we meet God. God has used the Scriptures to reveal to us the divine purpose for all of creation and for the Divine Personality. Reading, meditating on, and praying on the Scriptures open a window to the Divine. In the Scriptures, we engage the self-revelation of God.

While I am not a literalist (I feel that language is more artful and poetic than most literalists would grant), I am not a slavish devotee of historical biblical criticism either. As far as I have been able to determine, much biblical criticism does little more than prove its own assumptions. For me, it is the very assumptions we hold about our existence that the Scriptures are meant to challenge and to unfold before us.

I treat the Scriptures more like poetry than prose. I am more interested in the underlying spiritual meaning than in proving historical accuracy or context. In the Scriptures, through the power of the Holy Spirit, we meet the living God. The Scriptures challenge us to look for the Divine Life in our life, to become aware of the Divine Life in our life, and to open our heart and mind so that we can be empowered by the Divine Life in our life.

I understand the role of story in the Scriptures much as the Orthodox Christians understand the role of the icon. The stories are a window, an avenue to the holiness of God, the nature of the created cosmos, and the life of the Spirit within the cosmos. The Scriptures are a window through which the Divine Life manifests itself to us and through which we see the Divine Manifestation.

I only hope that these meditations can appeal to the poet within us who marvels at life. God is the poet of the universe. The word *Creator* in our creeds is the English translation of the word *poieo* in the Scriptures, literally translated as "poet." So God is the Poet of all, and the way to comprehend God as Spirit is not "literally" but "poetically."

Throughout the centuries, one of the central paths to holiness has been meditating on the sacred Scriptures. The Benedictines, among others, call this *lectio divina*, or sacred reading. This is not reading primarily for knowledge of the mind, but reading from and for the heart. In this book, I will be giving suggestions on how to meditate on the Scriptures, either by the meditative repetition of biblical phrases or by imaginatively entering into biblical stories. Both ways of meditating are very traditional.

The use of repeated phrases may lead people into a deeper meditative state in which they may experience what they are saying in a deeper way. The same is true for using the imagination to explore scriptural stories. You may prefer one way over the other. Only you will know what is best for you. Some of you may be led into a special spiritual realm of joy and delight, others may experience new truths. There is no right experience.

A Word About Meditating

In order to meditate optimally, you need to find a quiet place, away from distractions. You may have to get up early in the morning or wait until late evening to do this if you live in an active community or family.

Sit comfortably and quietly: so comfortably that you will not want to move for the time period you have set for yourself, and so quietly that even your movements will not disturb your mental processes. Some people enjoy standing. Some can even lie down without falling asleep. Please keep in mind that the goal is to increase awareness, not to fall asleep. Informing others of what you are doing may help them respect your quiet and not interrupt except for an emergency. I prefer to meditate either early in the morning or late at night because it is usually quieter, and there are fewer distractions. I also recommend using as soft a light as possible.

Try not to worry about distractions. You will be distracted from within and from outside. If you are distracted, just be aware of it, and return to the focus of your meditation. Our minds are constantly active, and the point of meditation is to calm that activity and learn to focus it. Just return to your meditation. In time you may become more adept at focusing your mind. Do not try, however, to be perfect in meditation. Success in meditation is showing up and trying to do it.

I will invite you to do some exercises that you may feel uncomfortable doing. If so, don't do them. If you choose to skip an exercise, fine. Do what you can. I will also be asking you to contribute your experiences to the process. At the end of each meditation, several suggestions will be made for you to use as you wish.

Before you begin these eleven meditations, you may want to read the Resurrection stories in the closing chapters of each of the Gospels. This would give you an overview of the biblical materials that are the basis of this book. This would include chapter 28 of Matthew, chapter 16 of Mark, chapter 24 of Luke, and chapters 20 and 21 of John. You might also want to use an edition of the Bible that has the sayings of Jesus highlighted in red ink, or consider highlighting Jesus' words with a highlighter pen. This will help you see the Resurrection sayings of

Jesus clearly. I also recommend reading chapter 15 of the First Letter to the Corinthians that was quoted at the beginning of this introduction.

Let Us Begin

By meditating on the last words of the resurrected Christ, I believe that we can recover the vital source of energy that made the early church what it was: a community that had experienced the living, resurrected Christ, took its self-understanding and direction from the words and presence of the resurrected Christ, and received power to become the community that would lead people to experience the presence of the resurrected Christ.

Meditation 1

Meeting the Resurrected Christ

The Words

The angel said to [Mary Magdalene and the other Mary], "Do not be afraid; I know that you are looking for Jesus who was crucified. He is not here; for he has been raised, as he said. Come, see the place where he lay. Then go quickly and tell his disciples, "He has been raised from the dead, and indeed he is going ahead of you to Galilee; there you will see him." So they left the tomb quickly with fear and great joy, and ran to tell his disciples. Suddenly Jesus met them and said, "Greetings!" And they came to him, took hold of his feet, and worshiped him. (Matthew 28:5–9)

Opening prayer. Risen Jesus, come and meet us face to face. Amen.

Reflection

Imagine the women hurrying away from the tomb, deeply bewildered. On the one hand they are filled with fear. What have his enemies done to Jesus? Where is the body? Are they going to further abuse his body? They had seen an angel, but was their experience real? Were they just dreaming? Enough had already gone wrong. Now what was going on? Yet they were also filled with joy. What if what the angel said was true? Could he really be alive? If so, it was too joyous to imagine.

The Bible tells us that "suddenly Jesus met them." How did he appear? What form did his resurrected body take? They did recognize him. Even so, the key point is not how he met them, but *that* he met them. The Greek for "met" means "drew near." Jesus met the women face to face. He drew near to them, expressing a definite intention on his part to come close to these beloved women.

He simply says, "Greetings" or "Hi." The word in Greek is the familiar form of greeting, the kind of greeting that someone would say a hundred times a day when running into people on the street, in the office, or out on the beach. He says just a simple "Hi."

Jesus, the crucified, the beaten, the insulted, the wonder worker, the healer, the brilliant rabbi. Jesus, the resurrected Christ, meets those he loves in the garden path and simply says, "Hi." The divine familiarity! The friendly gesture! One almost has to wonder what was going through his mind as he saw them coming up the pathway toward him. Was he thinking, "I should go at this gently. They look so disturbed, so confused, so hurt"? He must have known what a shock it would be to them to see him again. I can't help but think that he must have been a little amused at the incongruity of the situation. Here he was, the human being who had died, now living and about to interact with other humans who simply would not comprehend what had happened. So he says, "Hi."

Thus the divine self-revelation begins! They have met the resurrected Christ face to face. The encounter of humans with the Divine enters another chapter. As the new story begins, the humans are utterly amazed, fall on their faces, and worship him. They have met the resurrected Christ!

This simple meeting in the garden after the Resurrection is momentous in its effect and importance. Christ had suffered a horrible death, and the disciples were scattered, hiding in fear. They thought that they had been abandoned by God. Now with this simple greeting in the garden, all that has changed. The resurrected Christ is present. They meet him face to face. God is present.

The question this raises for us is, "Have we ever met the resurrected Christ?" Another way of asking the same question is, "How do we come to know the resurrected Christ?"

Certainly, prayer, Bible study, and the Holy Eucharist are some of the ways that we come to know the resurrected Christ. What are some others? Experiencing the power and presence of Christ in spiritual healing, and in the love of Christian community, or in the deep dedication of loving people to ministry in the world, or meeting the resurrected Christ in the life of others as they live lovingly and vibrantly in the presence of God, or also, meeting the resurrected Christ, the ruler of all creation, through the glory of the created order. These are just a few of the ways that we can meet the resurrected Christ. However the question remains, "How do we come to know the resurrected Christ"?

The Experience of Light in Meditation

Our face-to-face encounter with the resurrected Christ can begin by meditation. By opening the consciousness in this way, experiencing Christ as light and seeing our day-to-day existence in a new light become possible.

In the Exodus stories, God leads the people in the form of a pillar of fire. Moses experiences God appearing in the intense light of the burning bush. In the Transfiguration story in chapter 9 of Luke, the disciples report that when they saw Jesus with Moses and Elijah, Jesus' clothes and countenance shown brightly.

In the Resurrection stories, it is no accident that the angel at the tomb was shining brightly. The encounter with the lightsome angel just before meeting Jesus in the garden is expressive of the connection between the experience of light and the meeting with the Holy One. All through the Hebrew Scriptures and the Christian Testament, people experience the presence of God, the glory of God, and the holiness of God in the experience of light. So it happens in meditation that the resurrected Christ may be experienced as light.

To meet the light of Christ means that we see in a different way. It is the type of seeing we have when we encounter the beauty of a crocus emerging from frozen loam or when we behold for the first time the beauty of a newborn child. When we intentionally and attentively look at someone or something, we usually see them more completely. When meditating, we take time to stop and entertain something, and we then see it in a new light.

I learned to look intentionally through taking photographs. When taking photographs, you need to examine how the light is falling on or affecting the subject. You might even elaborately light the subject to bring out the features more clearly or maybe even to diminish features that need minimizing. Even today, I am often surprised when someone says to me, "Why are you looking at me so intently?" I then realize that I am looking at them intentionally with an eye to seeing them.

I also taught photography to children at one point to help them to see the beauty that surrounds them. We often take for granted what we see when we are only casually glancing at the world about us.

A priest friend of mine, a spiritual mentor, once said that it is not in going to church or in saying the liturgy that we experience God, but our mind is transformed into a different state than that of our normal cognition when we are in church during the liturgy and we see the light, we experience the luminosity of God pervading all things. Meditating is a way to intentionally put ourselves into the presence of the Risen Christ, this new light.

Spiritual Exercises

• Meditate, using your imagination, on the meeting between Jesus and the women. If it helps you, go to the Bible and read the entire story in chapter 28 of Matthew. Imagine Jesus in his risen body speaking to you and saying "Hi." What would you say to him? What would he say to you? Enter into dialog with the Risen Christ (some people find that writing the dialog aids them).

• Stand in a brightly lit room or even outdoors in the sunlight. Face the sun if you wish. Allow the sun to bathe you with its light and power. Meet the sun in this way, and enjoy its presence warmly flowing over you. Imagine meeting Jesus Christ, the sun of righteousness, and how it would feel.

• While standing, imagine that you are surrounded by an all-embracing light. Starting above your head, and working your way down over your entire body, encircle your whole self with your hands about two to three inches from your body. Imagine you are wrapping yourself in an envelope of light. Then stand up straight and bask in the presence of this light envelope that you have made for yourself. If you feel inclined, repeatedly pray, "Christ, Light."

• Lying flat on your back on the floor, imagine that you are dead and in the grave. Then imagine that you are being filled with light and being lifted up out of the grave, and transformed into a living creature of light. Stand up, and lift your hands outstretched in a prayer position. Let your body be filled with light, and radiate the light out around you.

• Sing a favorite hymn about Christ's or God's light.

Closing prayer

O gracious Light,
pure brightness of the everliving [God],
O Jesus Christ, holy and blessed!

Now as we come to the setting of the sun,
and our eyes behold the vesper light,
we sing your praises, O God: Father, Son, and Holy Spirit.

You are worthy at all times to be praised by happy voices,
O Son of God, O Giver of life,
and to be glorified through all the worlds.
Amen.

(The Book of Common Prayer, p. 118)

Greetings

Meditation 2

Christ's Gift of Courage

The Words

"Then Jesus said to them, 'Do not be afraid'" (Matthew 28:10).

Opening prayer. Risen Jesus, be with us as we meet our fears, and teach us that we need fear only the loss of you.

Reflection

One can only imagine how Mary Magdalene and Mary felt on first seeing Jesus in his resurrected state. They had gone to the tomb to anoint him and found the tomb empty. They then met him on the path in the garden—alive! Such a dramatic reversal of expectation would shock and horrify anyone. Terror, awe, joy, and confusion must have stormed within them.

Just as he had done throughout his ministry, Jesus sees their troubled heart, their confused and perplexed mind, and reassures them with the words, "'Do not be afraid,'" "'It is all right,'" "'Be assured that all is well.'" In other Gospel stories, Jesus is reported to have done and said the same sort of things. His whole life had been dedicated to healing people, inviting them to love and hope.

In Luke's account of the Resurrection, Christ asks his disciples, "'Why are you frightened?,'" (Luke 24:38). In John, he asks Mary Magdalene, "'Why are you weeping?'" (John 20:15). In both cases, Jesus wants to reassure his distraught disciples. He also wants them to look into their heart and examine the source of their fears and the substance of their faith.

In the story from Luke, Christ has suddenly appeared to a group of the disciples in Jerusalem. They are shocked at his sudden appearance, as though out of thin air, and he tries to reassure them. In the story in the Gospel of John, Jesus is posing the question to Mary Magdalene, who has remained at the tomb after Peter and John have come and gone, after the women had told them about their experience.

The resurrected Christ wants his frightened followers to put aside their paralyzing fear. And, indeed, the disciples needed to be reassured. Not only were they confused and perplexed at Jesus' reappearance, they were terrified about the political situation in which they found themselves. Jesus had been crucified as a criminal and a blasphemer. He had been condemned as a seditionist and a revolutionary. His followers were placed in the same boat. If they were to be found, they feared that their lives would be of no account. What with the rage and jealousy of the established religious authorities and the reprisals of the government, they had plenty to fear.

Because they really had not yet assimilated the predictions of Jesus about his own death and Resurrection, the disciples had little reason to believe that anything good was going to come out of the recent events. Nevertheless Jesus says to them, "'Do not be afraid.'" The word for not in Greek is a very strong form for the negative. So, in effect, he declares, "Do not have any fear!" It is as much a command as it is a reassurance.

Once when racing on my sailboat, we were suddenly hit with a severe thunderstorm and squall. The high winds tore at the boats' sails and broke the riggings on some of the boats. The sails on one of the boats were torn to tatters, failing loose fabric in the wind. Fear filled my crew. Some of them froze, others reacted by panicking. They looked for commands from the skipper as to what to do and how to do it. They sought a calm, authoritative word from the skipper so that they could act effectively to save the boat. They also wanted to know that they were going to be all right.

We managed to get the large foresail (the jib) down due to the heroics of a young man who leapt forward to the deck. I managed to orient the boat in such a way as to reduce the effect of the wind on the rigging and the mainsail. We survived with little damage and even completed the race.

I remembered later how we reflected on the excitement of the moment and the quick action that we needed to save the sails, the boat, and ourselves. We commended ourselves for knowing what to do and for doing it quickly. Later when the adrenaline ceased pumping through my body, I gave thanks to God for not losing my cool and for being able to give clear, definite commands. The quick, sure response under pressure by the crew made saving the boat possible, and this gave us all the confidence that the situation could be managed. When Jesus told his disciples, "'Do not be afraid,'" I surmise that he reassured them with his admonition and gave them reason to believe that all would work out well.

In this gentle, but firm, reassuring command Jesus is saying two things clearly: God is in charge, and we human beings need not panic or fear that the ship of life is about to be destroyed. Jesus is saying something about the very nature of life and of God: There is no reason to fear. Especially now that I have been raised from the dead, God's loving will has been victorious. As Saint Paul says later, "[Neither] height, nor depth, nor anything else in all creation, will be able to separate us from the love of God in Christ Jesus" (Romans 8:39). There is, thus, nothing to fear. We need fear no one. The powers of death and hell have been vanquished.

Meeting Our Fears

One of the side effects of doing regular meditation is coming to know and meet our fears and anxieties. When we meditate, the things that are bothering us are constantly on the surface of our consciousness. Some arise from our day-to-day affairs, others come up from the depths of our psyche. If we meditate regularly, keeping in mind the assurance of the Risen Christ, we cannot fail to confront our fears and begin to deal with them.

The word for anxiety used in the Christian Testament is *merimnao.* It literally means "running around in the mind or memory." Anxiety is "the monkey on our back." The Risen Christ invites us to eventually face the monkeys on our back, the demons from within, our fears or anxieties.

Meditating or attending to our fears with the grace of the Risen Christ helps us to face our anxieties, become acquainted with them, and be victorious over them. A life that includes regular meditation, like a life that includes regular physical exercise, helps us learn how to observe all that goes on within us with a spirit of reassurance and calm. We learn how to "not be afraid."

I have long had the dream of solo ocean sailing. Entering into the open sea in a small sailing boat can thrill and terrify. Leaving Narragansett Bay and entering the ocean, riding the ocean swells, the rollers, as they are first felt under the boat, is an incomparable thrill. For a long time, however, my fear of dying kept me from accomplishing my dream of sailing alone on the ocean.

I still have a fear of the ocean. A person would have to be a fool not to fear the power of the sea. Belief in the grace of the Risen Christ, however, has given me more courage and alleviated some of my fear of dying. I now have sailed by myself on the ocean and even sailed a single-handed ocean race.

Just recently this overcoming of fear was severely tested when I lost a mast in a heavy storm out in Vineyard Sound. One small part of the boat broke and caused the mast to fold like an accordion. A month after losing the mast, I was scheduled to be in a single-handed ocean race. I wondered if I still had the courage. In prayer and meditation, the mysterious grace and blessed assurance came that the Risen Christ was with me. I could hear Christ reminding me, "Richard, fear not."

Spiritual Exercises

• Meditate for ten minutes each day over a period of several days. Listen to your inner self. Listen to the noise ("the monkey on your back"). What are you afraid of? After meditating, write down what your noise was. What are the underlying fears that you are dealing with? fear of death? fear of loss? fear of loving someone? Take your fears to Christ, and ask him to bless them and to transform them. Do not be afraid to ask for Jesus' help in dealing with your fears.

• Openly share your fears with a person or persons you trust. Sort out which fears are healthy (like respect for the power of the sea) and which are toxic. Seek your confidants' support and reassurance. Let them be Christ to you, with their understanding and reassurance. Then try to face your fear— do what your fear keeps you from doing—and see what happens. You may be surprised.

• Sit quietly, eyes closed, body relaxed. Rest the palms of your hands facedown on your thighs. Remember the presence of the Risen Christ telling you not to be afraid, and imagine dropping your fears into his hands. Talk to Christ about each fear, each monkey on your back, then hand it over to him.

Then turn your hands over so that the palms face upward. In this receptive position, ask Christ to open your heart to his grace—whatever grace you need to not be afraid, to let go of fear, to rest in his blessed reassurance.

End the meditation with the Lord's Prayer or spontaneous thanks and praise.

• If you know either "Be Not Afraid," by Robert J. Dufford, or "How Can I Keep from Singing?," sing the hymn slowly, reflecting on Christ's words. Or sing any hymn that speaks to your fears and the assurance of the Risen Christ.

Closing prayer. Jesus Christ, courage and perseverance brought you through your darkest hours and into the Resurrection light. Calm our fears and still our anxieties as you calmed the waters of the sea and stilled the voices of detraction and discord, so that we might serve you in peace and quietness, ever mindful of your most holy life. In your blessed name, we pray. Amen.

Fear not

Meditation 3

Christ's Gift of Well-Being

The Words

When it was evening on that day, the first day of the week, and the doors of the house where the disciples had met were locked for fear, . . . Jesus came and stood among them and said, "Peace be with you." After he said this, he showed them his hands and his side. Then the disciples rejoiced when they saw the Lord. Jesus said to them again, "Peace be with you." (John 20:19–21)

Opening prayer. Risen Jesus, grant us your peace. Amen.

Reflection

Fear stymies living. Filled with fear, we cannot move physically or spiritually. However, Jesus gave his disciples a positive gift. He enabled them to enter into the reality of *shalom*, the reality of "peace."

According to the Gospel of Luke, the Messiah brings peace on earth and guides us into the pathways of peace. At the birth of John the Baptist, Zechariah is filled with the Holy Spirit and prophesies that John will be the harbinger of the one who is to come, the Messiah who will lead his people into *shalom* (Luke 1:79). Luke also has the angels proclaim, at the birth of the Messiah, "Glory to God in the highest heaven, / and on earth peace among those whom he favors" (Luke 2:14). The Messiah will bring the favor of God upon people of good will.

As Jesus enters Jerusalem, the voices in the crowd, responding to the miracles they had seen, shout out,

Blessed is the king
who comes in the name of the Lord!
Peace in heaven
and glory in the highest heaven.

(Luke 19:38)

And, finally in Luke, Jesus enters the room with the disciples and says to them, "'Peace be with you'" (Luke 24:36). The Messiah of the prophesies comes and brings the gift of peace— earthly peace and heavenly peace.

The resurrected Christ is recorded as saying the same thing in the same situation in the Gospel of John (20:19). But, in the Gospel of John, even before his death and Resurrection, Jesus tells the disciples not to be afraid (14:27). He warns them that they should be prepared for the worst, a warning that they little understood at the time: "'I have said this to you, so that in me you may have peace. In the world you face persecution. But take courage; I have conquered the world!'" (John 16:33). Obviously, when they are gathered in fear and disbelief in the room following Jesus' Crucifixion, Jesus' warnings and reassurance had little effect on them. They had yet to experience the "peace of God."

When Jesus came into the room and said, "'Peace be with you!'" Jesus' risen presence caused the disciples finally to experience the peace that they had only heard about earlier. Jesus had passed over into the new life, the resurrected life, so now his words had the power and effect that they did not have before. Jesus had been brutally crucified, and his radical love was manifested to them. The resurrected body of Jesus included the scars of the nails and the spear, as Thomas so needed to see. But here Christ was inviting them to peace.

The resurrected presence of Christ made the difference. Surely the disciples had been acquainted with death before this. Some of them had probably seen bloody deaths at the hands of the Romans. Indeed they had gathered in fear because they knew that they were wanted men and women. They may have feared one another also. After all one among them had betrayed Jesus. Judas had not returned, and it was rumored that he had taken blood money and fled. Peter had denied Jesus. So could anyone be sure of the others? Were there still more spies in the midst of the disciples?

Despair haunted their gathering. Everything that they had hoped for was now in ruins. They thought Israel was to be restored to a free state, and Jesus, their leader, was dead. Some had believed that he was the Messiah. Now he was gone. He could not be the Messiah, and he could not bring about a successful change in the political situation for the Jews. Where was justice? Where was peace? There was no hope.

When Jesus appeared in the room with them and uttered the words, "Peace be with you," everything changed. Death no longer held power over them. The authorities no longer needed to be feared. With Jesus' forgiveness and presence, they could forgive one another and again trust in God. Their hope was restored. The world had not changed, but they had changed. With Jesus' Resurrection, their resurrected living could now begin. All that they hoped for was resurrected. Despair and death were conquered, and they were alive and all was well. They experienced a deep inner peace that comes with knowing that "all is well."

When the Risen Christ said, "Peace be with you," he was announcing the end of an old world and an old way of living and perceiving. He was inviting the disciples to join with him in the victory and to enter with him into the new world, the world of "the peace of God, which surpasses all understanding" (Philippians 4:7). This time they understood. This time they heard. And this time they experienced exhilaration and joy at living again with Jesus.

The Peace of the Risen Christ in Meditation

Whatever one calls the process—centering, meditating, or contemplative prayer—one of the results of meditation can be a discovery of a deep sense of peace and well-being. Such peace is not cheaply or easily gained, and it is finally given to us always as a gift.

Indeed, like the fearful disciples, coming to peace can be difficult, fraught with all forms of emotional blocks—fear, frustration, anxiety, preoccupation, self-centeredness, laziness, guilt, and numerous other kinds of emotions—that keep us from enjoying just resting in God and in ourselves as good and well.

To find such peace, the focus has to be on the presence of the Risen Christ in our life. Such peace cannot come from "navel gazing" or introspection alone. For years I have used one form of meditation that has blessed me in many ways—the Jesus Prayer of the Orthodox tradition: "Lord Jesus Christ, Son of God, have mercy on me, a sinner." It constantly teaches me to focus only on the presence of Christ Jesus and to remember that there is no such thing as success and that we should not try for any kind of religious experience.

Such is the indirect way that peace comes into the soul and into our life as a gift. Ultimately *shalom* comes as a grace. We are like the disciples. Only when the resurrected Christ enters the room and speaks the word of peace to them are they given the gift of peace. In meditation we simply dispose ourselves to receive Christ's peace. We invite Christ into our soul.

The peace of God is often preceded by some death-unto-the-self. We give up trying to have an experience of God and let go of all the flurry of activity that goes on in our head, all the cares and worries that flood in. We invite our real self to be present to God, the self that God knows is completely dependent on the Divine Lover, the good Creator. Stripped of our need to control and our superfluous anxieties, we die to the false self and open our self to a new life experience of peace and well-being.

Meditating with the Risen Christ allows us finally to begin dealing with our own death—both the physical dying and the spiritual struggle for comprehension, belief, and peace. As we meditate on the Risen Christ, do we believe that he has in fact conquered death? Will we truly rise with him? Will all be well?

The peace of God has to be reborn in us daily by the spirit of God, when we open our heart, mind, and soul to God's grace.

Spiritual Exercises

• Find a quiet place, and meditate for at least twenty minutes. Relax into quiet. Breathe deeply and slowly. As noise and distractions come to your attention, gently acknowledge them, and then let them go. Listen with the ear of your heart to whatever the spirit of God has to say.

• Meditate using the words that Jesus said to his disciples, "Peace be with you." Pray the phrase slowly and quietly. If you lose concentration, you can whisper it.

• Meditate on your own dying. First recall the presence of the Risen Christ who wishes you peace. Then dialog with him about these questions:
  ○ Jesus, did you really conquer death?
  ○ Will I rise with you?
  ○ Will all be well?
  Listen for Christ's answers.

• Do an examen of consciousness with this question: How do I bring the peace of Christ to other people?

• In moments throughout the day, pray the Jesus Prayer: "Lord Jesus Christ, Son of God, have mercy on me, a sinner." Let it speak to your soul, realizing that Christ has already had mercy on you, but you may not have let Christ's grace and peace come into your soul.

Closing prayer

The peace of God, which passeth all understanding, keep your hearts and minds in the knowledge and love of God, and of his Son Jesus Christ our Lord; and the blessing of God Almighty, the Father, the Son, and the Holy [Spirit], be amongst you, and remain with you for always. Amen. (*The Book of Common Prayer*, p. 339)

Meditation 4

Christ's Gift of Enlivening Power

The Words

"[Christ] breathed on them and said to them, 'Receive the Holy Spirit'" (John 20:22).

Opening prayer. Risen Jesus, inspire us with your life-giving spirit. Amen.

Reflection

"'Receive the Holy Spirit.'" With these words, Jesus empowers his disciples. He breathes on them. His spiritual essence is conveyed to them out of the source of his eternal, resurrected person. In the same way that God spoke the word in the beginning of Creation when all the heavens and earth were made and all creatures and life came into being, so now Jesus breathes on the disciples. They are empowered to live the new, eternal life within created life.

In almost all of the Gospels and in the Acts of the Apostles, as Christ is leaving the disciples, he promises to send the Holy Spirit to them, and, with the power of the Spirit, they will carry on the work that up to then had been put only in his hands.

In the Gospel of Luke, Jesus says, "'And see, I am sending upon you what [God] promised; so stay here in the city until you have been clothed with power from on high'" (24:49).

In the Acts of the Apostles, Jesus says:

> While staying with them, [Jesus] ordered them not to leave Jerusalem, but to wait there for the promise of [God]. "This," he said, "is what you have heard from me; for John baptized with water, but you will be baptized with the Holy Spirit not many days from now. . . ."
>
> "You will receive power when the Holy Spirit has come upon you; and you will be my witnesses." (Acts 1:4–8)

Jesus expected God to empower the disciples to carry on the ministry that he had started. He even says he expects them to do greater works than he did (John 14:12). Now, after the Resurrection, Christ tells the disciples that they will be empowered from on high, and that they will be even more able to carry on the ministry of proclaiming the Good News of God and buoying up the brokenhearted. Indeed, with the coming of the Holy Spirit at Pentecost, the disciples preach powerfully, heal effectively, and perform many other acts that are signs that God was acting through them.

We read these accounts, probably believing that indeed those early disciples were filled with God's spirit. But do we expect such empowerment today? Do we believe that the Holy Spirit can change our life and work through us to do God's work in the world? Do we expect such things to happen in our life?

I gained new perspective on these questions through a recent conversation that turned to the question, "Why don't we expect the Holy Spirit to act today in the same way as in the time of the Apostles?" Once the question was asked, we recalled and recounted stories of people who we had seen being healed, not always instantly, but healed. People who had great fears began to live in the peace of God. People who had specific needs and asked for help, received the help they needed.

We realized that we still see people today expressing the love of God to those near them, even to their enemies.

In my ministry I have seen even more drastic healings. I have seen prayer make people well. I have heard doctors say, "It's a miracle," when they had given up, having done all that they could do. Indeed the Holy Spirit still works today. When we believe, when we pray, when we truly submit our spirits to God's spirit, amazing things happen in our life. We are empowered and changed by the Spirit. We are healed by the Risen Christ acting through the Spirit.

One way I remind myself of the source of all life, healing, and power is by offering thanks before meals. This way I do not take for granted something so basic as God's gift of food. I figure that if I take food for granted, then I will start taking for granted even larger gifts. All things come from God, and all things are being enlivened by God. Earthly life and eternal life are miracles. "Receive the Holy Spirit," Jesus says, and the miracle of life, the gift of eternal life are given.

The Enlivening That Comes

At one point in my life after being ordained and living for many years as a priest and doing what priests are meant to do—pray—I decided to take a vacation from prayer for a few weeks to see what would happen. It had been my practice to pray twice a day, morning and evening. I would read morning prayers, meditate, and pray my intercessory prayer list in the morning, and in the evening I would read something spiritual, then read the Bible (usually the Gospels), meditate briefly, and go to sleep.

However I was burned out, tired, and even a little irritated with the church during one period in my life. So I decided to take a spiritual holiday. I even decided not to go to church on Sunday for two weeks, but instead just got up, read the paper, and went about my daily schedule with no recognition of the fact that it was the day of Resurrection.

The results of this spiritual holiday were disastrous for me. First, I noticed that I was not as aware of God's presence in my life and in the life of others. Second, I found myself becoming more irritable, less compassionate, impatient, critical of others, and I ceased to see the glory of God in people and in the rest of nature, like my cat and the flowers and birds around the house. I also found myself more apt to fall prey to the very things that I find repugnant in our culture: watching too much television, eating too much, and generally becoming lazy and self-centered (even more so than when I am regular in prayer).

I would never suggest that just because I pray I am virtuous. Unfortunately for my family and friends I am still short on virtue. So while I did not abandon my practice of giving thanks before eating, things were even worse than usual.

But as mentioned above, my awareness of God acting in me and others was drastically reduced. This minivacation from God, the church, and prayer did convince me of one thing. I need God, the church, and prayer to continue to live in the awareness of the new life that had been given to me by the Risen Christ.

It would be simplistic to say that those who don't pray and go to church regularly cannot have experience of God. I am sure they do because God can be richly experienced through creation and events that happen to a person. Prayer and practice, however, are necessary for me to maintain my perspective that all life is a miraculous gift of God and to avoid falling back into a self-centered way of living.

The practice of prayer and meditation are extremely important to maintain if one is going to experience God as the giver of all life. The Nicene Creed says, "I believe in the Holy Spirit, the Lord, and giver of life." The term used here for "life" does not simply mean biological living, it means "real life," "quality of life," and even "eternal life" in the Scriptures. God is the source of the enlivening of all life. Prayer and meditation help us live in the spirit of the Risen Christ.

Spiritual Exercises

• Meditate using the phrase said by Jesus to his disciples, "'Receive the Holy Spirit.'" As you meditate, be aware of your breathing and say the phrase slowly as you inhale. Then say nothing as you exhale. Alternate inhaling using the phrase and exhaling saying nothing. Following the meditation, be aware of the inspiration and power that you have experienced.

• While standing, chant the following hymn on one note—any note that is comfortable for you to sing:

Come Holy Ghost, our souls inspire,
and lighten with celestial fire.

Thou the anointing Spirit art,
who dost thy sevenfold gifts impart.

Thy blessed unction from above
is comfort, life, and fire of love.

Enable with perpetual light
the dullness of our blinded sight.

Anoint and cheer our soiled face
with the abundance of thy grace.

Keep far our foes, give peace at home:
where thou art guide, no ill can come.

Teach us to know the Father, Son,
and thee, of both, to be but One,

that through the ages all along,
this may be our endless song:

Praise to thy eternal merit,
Father, Son, and Holy Spirit.

(*The Hymnal 1982*, no. 503)

• Pray to the Holy Spirit for the power to speak the Good News in your daily life.

• When Jesus sent the Holy Spirit, he "breathed" on his disciples. In the story of Pentecost, the Spirit comes with the wind, with air. We can go for some days without food, but we die quickly without air or breath. Just as breathing gives life to the body, the breath of the Spirit gives life to the soul. One way of attending to the gift of life—earthly life and eternal life—is to pay attention with a grateful heart to our breathing. Sit quietly. Close your eyes. Meditate on your breathing. In your mind's eye watch your breath as it comes in and slowly goes out. If you become distracted, simply let go of the distraction and return to watching your breath flow in and out, giving you life, the miraculous gift from God.

Closing prayer

Spirit Divine, attend our prayers,
and make this house thy home;
descend with all thy gracious powers,
O come, great Spirit, come. Amen.

(The Hymnal 1982, no. 509)

Meditation 5

Christ's Gift of Trust in God

The Words

"'Do not doubt but believe. . . . Have you believed because you have seen me? Blessed are those who have not seen and yet have come to believe'" (John 20:27–29).

"Oh, how foolish you are, and how slow of heart to believe all that the prophets have declared! Was it not necessary that the Messiah should suffer these things and then enter into his glory? . . ."

"Why are you frightened, and why do doubts arise in your hearts? Look at my hands and my feet; see that it is I myself." (Luke 24:25–26,38–39)

Opening prayer. Risen Jesus, teach us to trust you. Amen.

Reflection

I love the scenes in which Jesus invites the disciples to trust in him, because I sense in Jesus just a little frustration and irritation. Jesus suffered a horrible death on the cross. He had told his disciples that he would be raised from the dead. But they were not ready to hear that yet. Only God knows what they thought Jesus meant when he told them that he would rise again. Even when Jesus appears to the disciples, they have trouble trusting their own faculties and believing him.

As part of retreats or ministry gatherings, I have often played "trust games" with youth and young adult groups. Many exercises are standard fare during these gatherings. For instance, a person can be asked to stand in front of another person, to stiffen his or her back and legs, and then fall straight backward into the arms of the person behind. Needless to say, the one falling would have to trust the person behind before falling into the catcher's arms.

When Jesus said to his disciples, "Believe in me" or "Trust me," he was not asking them to indulge in an intellectual assent to a formulated doctrine of the church. The church had not formed yet. Christ was asking them to trust and believe *him*, and to trust their experience. He had really risen from the dead, and they could trust him, trust themselves, trust one another, and trust God. It was no trick, no feat of smoke and mirrors. They were not seeing phantoms, and they were not dreaming!

Furthermore, Jesus was saying that they could trust God. God had been faithful. God had raised Jesus up as he said God would. God can be trusted, life can be trusted. In this trust game, Jesus is saying: "You need to trust me. If you fall into my arms, I will catch you."

The church calls this deep trust in God, faith. Faith means having a deeply trusting, personal relationship or, as Thomas Merton says, "faith is a communion with God's own light and truth." The word *believe* comes from the Latin word *credo*, meaning "to set my heart on." So faith has less to do with accepting the teachings of "the faith"—the doctrines of the church—and everything to do with a deep trust in God, setting our heart on God.

This is the kind of trust that comes to people when they first experience conversion. Conversion simply means that they now trust God, whereas before they did not. This kind of faith causes a radical change in attitude and perspective in the lives of people.

Trust, setting our heart on Christ, is at the core of the resurrected life. Jesus says, "Have you believed because you have seen me? Blessed are those who have not seen and yet have come to believe" (John 20:29). He tells us that to trust in God is to be blessed. I call this particular teaching the tenth Beatitude. The Gospel of Matthew lists nine Beatitudes. Only the Gospel of John gives this tenth one, and that, separately, during a Resurrection appearance. He not only tells us that those who have seen his Resurrection are blessed, but that those who later have trust in his Resurrection, even though they did not directly see him face to face, are equally blessed.

Belief in the Resurrection of Jesus Christ is what leads us into our own experience of resurrection, and this allows us to live the resurrected life.

Developing Deep Trust

According to Tradition, the Holy Spirit working in our heart is the source of this gift of deep trust in the Risen Christ. Through meditation, that trust can grow. In the process of meditating, we grow in conversion, that is, in changing our view of the world, so that we begin to see our life through God's eyes and purposes and not just our own.

Learning to trust God is rather like learning to trust other people. We have to spend time with them, get to know them better, and find out whether they are really trustworthy. In meditation, we spend time with God. We listen to God speak from within. Eventually, no matter what methods we use to meditate, we end up developing a relationship with God and opening ourselves to experience the trustworthiness and friendship of God.

As we grow in faith in God, we let our guard down and gradually we experience a willingness to change and grow in our attitudes and behavior. We experience our own frailty and contingency. We experience the eternity of God and the glory of God. Most of all, we grow in trust that God has a plan for us and the cosmos, and that the plan is only for good.

Many of us are injured in our ability to trust. The story of a friend of mine brought this sharply home to me. While very young, my friend had lost his little brother to illness. The family, friends, and neighbors of the family were asked for money to get needed medical assistance to the young boy before he died. No one came to their aid.

After his little brother died, everyone brought money to the funeral. My friend was enraged for years. He got into fights on the playground and grew incorrigible. He got into so many fights that a priest encouraged him to go into prize-fighting to work out his anger. He fought for a while, until his father, who was a heavy drinker, insisted that he quit the ring.

My friend drank heavily and continued to brawl his way through life. One day he was drinking in a bar when he got into an argument and was shot. He lay on the floor bleeding to death, his life passing before him. In those mysterious moments, he experienced both the judgment and unconditional love of God. He survived the shooting and, miraculously, came back into living. Today he attends church, trusts deeply in God, is beloved by his family and children, no longer drinks or gets into fights, and has a wonderful zest for life.

Obviously my friend's story is dramatic. Some, perhaps many, people go through their whole life without accepting Christ's love and learning to trust, but the Risen Christ never stops inviting us to stop doubting. His Resurrection is the ultimate guarantee that we can trust God.

Relationship with God requires decision and commitment, just as any other relationship does. When we decide to spend time regularly with God in meditation and prayer, we are committing ourself to a relationship that will lead to a lasting trust.

Spiritual Exercises

• Meditate on this question: "Is it easier for me to believe in Christ's Resurrection in glory or to believe in his suffering and death?" Converse with Christ about your answer.

• Do you play trust games with other people in which you test their trustworthiness or their faithfulness? Do you ever play trust games with God? Can you ever win these games?

• Think of someone you trust. What is it that allows you to trust that person? Imagine someone you do not trust. What is it that causes you to distrust that person? What have you learned about your ability to trust others? What makes one person trustworthy and another person not trustworthy?

• Review your life story, looking for instances in which you found that you could trust in God's love and Christ's promise that ultimately "all will be well." Then look for instances when your faith was weakened, maybe almost lost. Give thanks to God for times of trust, and ask for the grace you need to grow in faith in those circumstances that weaken your faith.

• Meditate for twenty minutes, being aware that you are in the presence of Christ. Repeat slowly, "I trust you, Risen Jesus."

• What simple steps could you take to more firmly set your heart on God and to trust in your sisters and brothers in Christ?

Closing prayer

O God of peace, who hast taught us that in returning and rest we shall be saved, in quietness and in confidence shall be our strength: By the might of [your] Spirit lift us, we pray [you], to [your] presence, where we may be still and know that [you are] God, through Jesus Christ. (*The Book of Common Prayer*, p. 832)

Believe

Meditation 6

Christ Forgiving and Healing

The Words

"'Thus it is written, that the Messiah is to suffer and to rise from the dead on the third day, and that repentance and forgiveness of sins is to be proclaimed in his name to all nations'" (Luke 24:46–47).

Opening prayer. Risen Jesus, come among us with your healing and forgiving presence. Heal us and make us whole. Amen.

Reflection

The proclamation of the Gospel is the proclamation of the wonderful mercy of God. Divine mercy always has the last word. After all it is Good News that is being announced. Certainly the Apostles needed Good News as they cowered together after the Crucifixion and then heard the shocking announcement of Christ's Resurrection.

How do you think the Apostles felt when they were in the upper room? Imagine how you would have felt after the events of Jesus' Crucifixion. Would you have been angry with God for letting you down, for abandoning you and Jesus? Would you have been feeling guilty that you had run away and cowered with fear? Would you have been suspicious of your friends, and wondered if any more of them were going to betray the group? Would you have been angry at Jesus for not making things work out all right? Would you expect to be punished by God for these thoughts and for the results of your actions? After all you were with him and did not lift a finger to save him.

Now Jesus comes into the room. He does not upbraid the disciples for their failure to follow him, for their lack of courage, or for their lack of trust in God. He simply says: "Hi," "Peace be with you," "Fear not," "Trust God," and "Receive the Holy Spirit." Christ brings peace rather than retribution. Christ offers reconciliation, forgiveness, and healing, instead of further judgment, condemnation, and death. After all, God's purpose in sending the Word was to heal creation. The word *healing* originated in an old Saxon word for hale or whole. Christ comes to make creation whole again. Certainly it has been broken.

Offering forgiveness and salvation is part of healing. Forgiveness makes whole a broken relationship. Salvation comes from a Greek word *sos*, meaning "to restore to wholeness or health." I like to think of it as the acronym for "save our ship," the old SOS code used in emergency situations. Forgiveness and salvation heal, make whole, restore health to individuals, to the community, to creation. Jesus brings forgiveness, salvation, healing to the disciples, but he goes a step further when he empowers them to proclaim forgiveness and salvation to the whole world.

Living the resurrected life therefore means two things: being aware of the divine compassion that pervades the cosmos, and being empowered by that compassion to be an instrument of forgiveness, salvation, and healing. Whenever we have compassion for the least creature or for another person, spiritual and physical healing can take place.

Healing ministry, therefore, is to be expected from Christians. We are called to mend creation. The Christian mission traditionally includes the ministries of medicine, hospitals, and education. These are expressions of the healing of bodies and minds that accompany the proclamation of the Good News. Christ says to us, "Go," "Preach," and "Heal!" The resurrected Christ tells his disciples that signs will accompany the preaching of the Gospel in his name. The sick will be healed, and demons will be expelled (Mark 16:16–18). Healing comes, even now two thousand years later.

A friend of mine called me the other day and said, "Do you believe in healing?" I was cautious in responding because I did not know why he was asking the question. As our conversation proceeded, he explained that he had been healed of cancer. He was told that he had little time to live and that an operation on his lungs was necessary to remove cancerous cells. The night before the surgery, he prayed deeply and felt reassured that he would be all right. When he was taken into surgery the next day, he had no cancerous cells in his body.

He called me because he knew another person who was sick with cancer, and he wanted to know if it was all right for him to go and pray with her. I told him I would go with him if he wanted me to, but if he had a close relationship with the sick woman, it would be fine if he went by himself. He had experienced a healing in his life and wanted to share his healing with another person who was similarly sick. I felt a bit sad that he would even have to call and ask my opinion. Of course he could and should go to pray with the person. As Christians, one of our deepest callings is to pray for the healing for one another and the world.

Forgiveness and Healing in Meditation

Crying while meditating is a common experience for many people for at least two reasons. First, during meditation the mercy, the kindness, and the compassion of God can be overwhelming. Second, the process of meditation opens our soul, enabling the Divine to act within us. At one period in my life, all I did when meditating was sit and weep. The experience was refreshing and exhilarating, my emotions seemed to be out in the open. I was weeping in the presence of God, and God simply accepted me and my weeping. I felt that my sins were being washed away by the mercy of God.

I suppose that I was weeping for my sins, but that would be overly simplistic. I wept because of my perception of the beauty of Holiness, on the one hand, and I wept because of the transitoriness of all life, on the other. Both of these experiences were so beautiful that I wept. During this same time, I was able to accept that someday I would die like all other creatures, but I knew that dying would not be the end. I would enter into the glory of God in a more full and complete way. My resurrection would take place. What joy! What glory!

Meditating is a process of healing. The process of meditation brings us more into living the resurrected life. It makes us aware of God's marvelous mercy, kindness, and forgiveness. It allows us to see ourselves as accepted, forgiven, and healed by God. We see ourselves as fragile and limited creatures, nonetheless, glorious ones in our own right. As we are forgiven and healed, we are able to forgive others. Divine healing takes place within us, and within the community of which we are a part, when we learn how to forgive our sins and the sins of others.

Spiritual Exercises

• Recall a time when you felt hurt. Who was it that hurt you? What were the circumstances? How did you feel? Now imagine that you are at the same time and place in which the hurt took place. Imagine Jesus with you and with the other person. Ask Jesus to heal your hurt, your grief, your pain, your anger. Ask Jesus what he feels about your hurt, what he feels for the person who hurt you, what he feels for you. If someone hurt you, ask Jesus to forgive that person, and to help you to forgive her or him.

If you wish, invite some good friends to pray with you. They could lay their hands on your head or shoulders and pray with you. Do not be afraid to take your hurt to Jesus to be healed. He will heal you if you ask him to do so.

• The above exercise can be repeated as you remember someone you have hurt. How do you feel about it? Invite Jesus into the scene. How does he feel about it? What would he tell you to do or to say to the person you hurt? Could you say it to the person? Could you write the person you hurt a note in which you ask for forgiveness and seek to heal the relationship? Could you ask for forgiveness face to face? Jesus gives us the power to retain or release sins, even our own. Can you forgive yourself? Can you experience the depths of Jesus' love for you and for the person you hurt?

• Everything we say and do affects someone either positively or negatively. We have the power to hurt or heal, to forgive or not, to touch someone lovingly or in a way that hurts them. A game that a friend taught me helps us to understand this. Give yourself twenty-five pennies, and a friend or your spouse twenty-five pennies. When you say something that encourages them, uplifts them, helps them, they give you a penny. If you say something negative, you give them a penny. They do the same with you. At the end of the day, converse with your partner in this exercise, using the pennies as symbolic indicators about the healing and hurting in your relationship. This can be a revealing exercise.

• Picture Jesus standing in front of you and meditate for twenty minutes on the phrase: "I forgive you, forgive others."

• This simple chanting meditation can help you touch your need for healing and God's constant readiness to grant it. Once you are relaxed and have reminded yourself that the Risen Christ is with you, close your eyes and chant quietly this ancient liturgical prayer: *Kyrie eleison, Christe eleison, Kyrie eleison* or Lord, have mercy. Christ, have mercy. Lord, have mercy. Meditate using it, chanting it slowly over and over. Invite each word into your soul. If you know one of the chant melodies for the Kyrie, certainly use it if you prefer.

• Do a thorough examination of conscience. List the areas of your life where you need forgiveness and healing. Then discuss each area with Christ. Ask for forgiveness and healing.

• Meditate on ways you can be a healing presence in a broken relationship; in a local, ailing ecosystem; at work; in your congregation. Take action.

Closing prayer. Risen Jesus, full of mercy and forgiveness, grant to us your compassion that we may be healed and become healing instruments to those near us. Teach us to be ready to forgive others, as we have been forgiven by you. Make our heart gentle that your mercy may be manifest in us. In your holy name, we pray. Amen.

Meditation 7

Living in Christ's Likeness

The Words

"[Jesus] said to [Peter], 'Follow me!'" (John 21:19)

> "Do not let your hearts be troubled. Believe in God, believe also in me. In [God's] house there are many dwelling places. If it were not so, would I have told you that I go to prepare a place for you? And if I go and prepare a place for you, I will come again and will take you to myself, so that where I am, there you may be also. And you know the way to the place where I am going." (John 14:1–4)

Opening prayer. Risen Jesus, my teacher, lead me in the way that you want me to go. Make teachable my heart, that I may become your student and so conform myself to you that I become a beacon of love to those around me. In your holy name, I pray. Amen.

Reflection

Following his Resurrection, Christ invites Peter and, by extension, the disciples to "Follow." Jesus' earthly journey was over, but his life continues. In this context, I surmise that he was inviting Peter to enter fully into the kind of life that he had modeled for Peter: a life of powerful ministry—healing, preaching the Good News, teaching, sacrificing, celebrating, and finally, Rising into glory.

In the passage from the Gospel of John (14:1–4) Jesus is trying to prepare his disciples for his death and Resurrection. First, he encourages them not to be worried. Then he tells the disciples that he will prepare a place for them in the mansion of God. Last, he invites them to "follow him." He is leading them into the spiritual realms, and so it is not surprising that the disciples do not understand what he is saying. They continue to interpret what he is saying to them in their own terms.

The meaning of *disciple* is "learner." The word for disciple in the Christian Testament comes from the Greek word *mathetes*. It is the same word from which we derive our English word *mathematics*, and it means a "structured system of learning." *Mathetes* were to follow a "master" who would show them the particular spiritual system that the master was expecting them to follow. So when Jesus says, "'I am the way, and the truth, and the life'" (John 14:6), he is saying, what I show you is *the way*—in Greek implying a specific practice or method that a teacher gave to the disciples that would lead them into spiritual understanding of *the truth*. This way to the truth will then lead the disciples to experience the *life*—the word in the Greek meaning "quality life," "life with God," or "eternal life." In short, Jesus is telling the disciples to follow him, the master, because he can lead them to resurrected life, life that has many more dimensions to it than we thought possible to live here and now.

Being human we need some shape to our new way of life, our following of Jesus. Traditionally, the Way of the Christian is given shape through study of the Christian Testament, worship, education, communal love, ministry, and evangelism.

First we study the Bible to encounter the person of the Risen Christ. Worship means that we regularly celebrate the Resurrection of Jesus Christ with the community, and we pray privately so that we grow in relationship with him. Education means that we seek to learn more about Jesus Christ by reading, talking, and listening to others who are further along the Way than we are. Communal love means that we relate to a community of those who trust in God and love one another. Ministry means that we use our powers and gifts for healing, forgiveness, and charity. Finally evangelism means that we share our trust in the Risen Christ with others.

With the grace of the Risen Christ, each Christian can do all these things, and thus begin to be disciples of Jesus who says, "Follow me!"

The Desire to Learn

Meditating daily often increases our thirst for spiritual knowledge and understanding of the Scriptures. It is hard when working full time and having multiple responsibilities to discipline ourselves to do regular spiritual reading. Often the day-to-day demands intervene. But we need to set aside the time to pray and study in order to become a wellspring of God's love. We cannot give to others what we do not possess ourselves.

Meditating regularly also brings us into a closer relationship with Jesus. Sometimes the relationship is even a little too close. Over the years I have feared to venture further because I might have to change. As was true for Jesus' disciples, his truth can make me quite uncomfortable. But, through prayer and inviting Jesus into my life, he becomes alive for me in a personal, fuller way. And as we know and follow him, we grow more into the image of "the Master."

One of my favorite television serials was *Kung Fu*. I especially liked the portions of the story that dealt with Grasshopper growing up under the instruction of his Chinese master teacher. The master trains Grasshopper in defensive exercises to ward off an attacker. He is amazed at the ability of his master who, though blind, can sense what is around him in an almost superhuman fashion. I marveled at the veneration that Grasshopper had for his master. After long training, Grasshopper is able to walk on flaming coals without pain or flinching. The essence of the program, however, was that in order to become a spiritual person one has to train.

People would think we were crazy if we told them that we were going to become champion figure skaters instantly, starting from scratch and without any coaching. And we would be crazy. Why then do so many of us think that we can be whole, holy, or wise without a teacher?

When I was very young, Jesus was a stranger to me, an almost fictional figure. When I began to learn more about the Bible and occasionally go to church, he became an acquaintance of historical importance, even a prophet or philosopher of great stature. When I began to study about Jesus in the Scriptures and meet him in meditation, he became my master. I had moved from being a stranger to being a disciple.

Of course I have had many relapses into old ways, and sometimes I struggle to follow him where he leads. So I continually attempt to discern him and his Way. Only through the graces of prayer, meditation, and the thirst to study have I grown at all. The Holy Spirit continues to work within me to lead me to follow the Way of the master.

Jesus invites us all to follow him. Dare we?

Spiritual Exercises

• In the presence of the Risen Christ, meditate for twenty minutes on the phrase, "Follow me."

• Study of the Scriptures, worship, education, community building, ministry, and evangelism are all Christian spiritual disciplines, that is, practices associated with being a disciple or follower of the Risen Christ. Do an examen of consciousness about your spiritual discipline using the following questions:
  ○ Do I regularly read, study, and pray with the sacred Scriptures?
  ○ How and with whom do I enter into public worship? How do I pray privately?

○ How and with whom do I learn ways to grow spiritually: prayer groups, Bible sharing groups, retreats, spiritual reading?

○ How do I demonstrate the love of God toward the community, friends, family, neighbors, coworkers, animals, plants, and other creatures? How do I define my community of love?

○ To whom do I minister? How do I bring healing to others?

○ With whom do I share my deepest convictions? Am I self-conscious about sharing the Good News?

• *Lectio divina,* or sacred reading and study, is an ancient form of Christian meditation. Most world religions make sacred reading an important part of their spiritual discipleship. The following exercise is one method of praying with the Scriptures or other spiritual books. Try this method of holy study using the passages from John at the beginning of this meditation or on any text. (Directions are given for solitary prayer, but the meditation can easily be adapted for use with a group.)

○ Center yourself and relax in silence for some time.

○ Slowly read the passage. Let your heart work through it, tasting words or phrases that seem to invite special attention.

○ Repeat over and over again one line that seems to be especially important for you. Let its import become clear to you.

○ Read the passage again—slowly, attentively.

○ In your mind and heart, formulate a one-word or short-phrase response to the reading. Recite the word or phrase in harmony with your breathing.

○ Slowly read the passage once again.

○ Ponder the reading with this question in mind: How does this reading touch my life at this particular time?

○ End with a quiet period, a prayer, the Lord's Prayer, or just thoughts of thankfulness.

Closing prayer. God of all creation and giver of all life, inspire us with your spirit that we may choose to follow wherever you lead us. Guide us in the pathways of knowledge and peace that we may truly be your disciples, daily grow more and more into your likeness, and finally dwell with you in life eternal. We ask this in your holy name. Amen.

Follow

Meditation 8

Feed My People

The Words

"When they had finished breakfast, Jesus said to Simon Peter, 'Simon, son of John, do you love me more than these?' He said to him, 'Yes, Lord; you know that I love you.' Jesus said to him, 'Feed my lambs'" (John 21:15).

Opening prayer. Risen Jesus, heavenly manna to your faithful, you feed us with yourself in the mystical meal you called us to share. Feed us daily with the gift of your nurturing love, so that we may know the love you have for us and share that love with others. In your holy name, we pray. Amen.

Reflection

Jesus tells Peter to follow him only after asking him three times, "'Do you love me?'" (John 21:15–18). Each time, Peter professes his love, and each time, Jesus tells him to take care of "'my sheep.'" These words to Peter have served as one of the church's calls to the ministry of pastoral care. In fact, we still use the word *pastoral*, reflecting the shepherding imagery that Jesus used. We are still being called to "pastor" one another, to love one another, to care for one another.

Before his Ascension, the resurrected Christ established a community of caring, intimacy, and love. According to traditional teaching the most important characteristic of the Christian community and of each individual Christian is that they care for one another, for people who are poor and outcast, and for the whole of God's creation. When one has experienced the love of God in such a deep, intimate way, then the obvious response to such love is to love others in the same way.

In 1 Corinthians 13:13, when Paul extols the three great virtues—faith, hope, and love—he makes sure that we all know clearly that "the greatest of these is love." And the one great sign that a community is really Christian in character is that the community members love one another. One of the final, and therefore possibly most important, conversations Jesus had with Peter as recorded in the Resurrection narratives was to remind him of the importance of committed communal, nurturing love.

Immediately before the Risen Jesus questioned Peter, he hosted a strange picnic on the shore of the Sea of Tiberias, where the disciples had been fishing unsuccessfully. Upon the advice of Jesus about where to cast their nets, the disciples caught more fish than they could handle. Jesus called out to them from the shore, "Bring some of the fish that you have just caught" (John 21:10). Then he invited them to "come and have breakfast" (John 21:12). Jesus once again showed what caring is about: giving people what they need—in this case, hospitably feeding them.

This scene causes me to remember scenes from my youth. Living on a lake, we fished a lot. We would often go out and catch a mess of bluegills and fry them up for dinner. My mother would say almost the same words to me that Jesus said to the disciples: "What did you catch?" "Oh, what a wonderful mess of bluegills! Come, bring them in when they're cleaned, and we'll cook them up right away for dinner." If we did not give what was not used to the neighbors, we froze the remainder for future dinners.

Just yesterday a neighbor of mine gave me some venison from last year's hunt. He had cooked up a special meal to share with his hunter friends, and he came over to give me a taste of the venison. He had cooked it according to his own special recipe. He has a deep relationship with the animal he has killed, and he has a deep relationship with his fellow hunters with whom he will share the meal.

These scenes of preparing and sharing a meal are primal and mystical. They call on all of our basic relationships: communal relationships of eating, of sharing the catch, and the sense of being at home and safe with food, not to mention expressing our intimate relationship and connectedness with nature.

Holidays are so special because we gather together as families. We talk with one another, catch up on what is happening in one another's life. We drink with one another. We prepare the food together. We cook one another's favorite recipes. Then we gather around the table, say grace, and participate in a wonderfully nourishing meal. Holiday meals, like the meals of fish and venison, are deeply primal expressions of our need for community, nourishment, and love.

Earthly hospitality reflects divine hospitality. Hospitality is an expression of our interconnectedness in divine love. As Christians who have experienced the resurrected life, every meal is a love feast, and our special meals even more so. When we sit down to eat, we not only sit down with one another; the whole universe is on our table in the form of bread, wine, fruits, vegetables, and the meat from God's creatures who coinhabit planet earth. In sharing a feast, we celebrate the Creator's gifts, and so the Creator. When all is said and done, any meal shared in hospitality is really a mystical party that we are attending, and we have a Divine Lover as our host. Those who are living a resurrected life know this and appreciate it.

Of course the celebration of the Last Supper, Communion, is a special, sacred expression of divine hospitality. The distribution of the gifts of bread and wine is the most sacred moment of the sacred rite. It is the moment when Jesus, who has invited us to the divine meal and who indeed has become the meal, feeds each of us with the heavenly eternal food, which is his resurrected body and blood. The bread we eat, and indeed

Jesus himself, is called the "host." Such spiritual feeding is the supreme act of hospitality in the universe, and it is expressive and inclusive of all acts of hospitality that happen in our daily life.

The resurrected Christ says to us, "Come and have breakfast." It is the invitation to the mystical meal of the spiritual universe of divine love. Can we refuse?

He also tells us, after being nourished by his life, "Feed my lambs." Can we refuse?

Experiencing Divine Love

Meditation or deep prayer has the effect sometimes of allowing us to experience the deep love God has for us. In turn, we experience love for other human beings and for the rest of creation. The love we experience may be compassion or forgiveness, but at times it comes into our heart in a more primal way, as wonder, awe, or a profound reverence. Words fail me, but many of us have a sense of this mysterious love. In the Christian Testament, the word most commonly used for love is *agape*. This word, uncommon in popular Greek usage, provides a unique focus to Christian love. *Agape* is love for the person in herself or himself. It is love for their very being. How a person behaves or how virtuous a person is has nothing to do with this kind of love. *Agape* is love simply for the being of the person, and it is the same with other creatures and things. *Agape* is our response to a pure gift of God's grace. God loves us this way and even gives us the grace to respond this way: to God, to one another, and to creation. We cannot earn *agape;* God gives it, and we either respond to it or refuse it.

One of my goals as a photographer is to take a subject, like a flower, isolate it, and try to capture its essential being on film. It is stunning to contemplate the essential beauty of one of God's creatures: animal, plant, or mineral. I often take creatures for granted. I lump them together by using their name: "cat," "giraffe," "centipede." Thousands upon thousands of creatures inhabit this planet, especially when we count the insect world. Many of these signs of God's love we have not met yet, at least not in person. When we do, once in a while we actually see and pay close attention to the wonder of their creation. Then we realize how fantastic, strange, and wonderful being alive really is.

This is why the words *reverence* or *respect* also fit as possible descriptions for *agape*. We have reverence or respect for something when we treat it as valued in and for itself, when we esteem it. At least for me, *agape* also comes to mean "awe." I stand in awe of the being of my children, of my life's mate, my family, and of each creature and object in the universe. Life, and all creation, is indeed "awe-full"—full of living creatures of which to be in awe. By helping us pay attention, meditation helps us to grow in this deep caring for one another and for the whole of God's creation.

If we would begin to reverence each human being and other of God's creatures, then we would not be in the mess we are in. Meditation and prayer can open the door to the experience of the wonder and awesomeness of each human being and creature of the universe. The invitation is open to us for a divine love feast, "Come and have breakfast." And what a feast!

Spiritual Exercises

• What nurtures you? having guests for dinner? listening to music? having parties or social gatherings? reading your favorite books? praying? taking trips to foreign lands? walking in the woods, in the mountains, or in the desert? sailing? Take stock of what nurtures you and make a plan to ensure that you receive nurturing in body, mind, and soul.

• How do you nurture your family and friends? cook? provide a home for your family? clean the house? go shopping with others for food or clothing? read to the children? take someone to the movies or to a play? hug someone? send a kind note to someone? play? bring home flowers? teach someone something that you know how to do well? Again do an inventory of the ways you nurture family and friends. Ponder your inventory and reform it as you can with God's grace.

• How do you nurture strangers and enemies? give money to charities? give volunteer time to a helpful organization? offer forgiveness to people who have hurt you? seek to correct some social ill that demeans people? Make a list of all the things you do to nurture strangers and enemies. Again meditate over your list and ask God's help to love more fully.

• Meditate on the phrases, "I love you" and "Feed my sheep." During the meditation, imagine Jesus Christ saying these phrases to you.

Closing prayer. Jesus Christ, holy friend, you fed your disciples the heavenly manna of your body and blood, and you met with them on the seashore and invited them to dine with you. Feed us now that we may never hunger or thirst again for the eternal life that you offer, and may we be so strengthened by your nourishment that we live and serve you and your creations all our days. We ask this in your holy name. Amen.

Love

Meditation 9

Returning to God

The Words

"Jesus said to [Mary], 'Do not hold on to me, because I have not yet ascended. . . . But go to my brothers [and sisters] and say to them, "I am ascending . . . to my God and your God"'" (John 20:17).

Opening prayer. Risen Jesus, it is in returning to and resting in you that we will be healed. Help us, we pray, to follow willingly as you lead us into the wholeness you want for each of us. Amen.

Reflection

At first Jesus' words to Mary Magdalene might seem strange. She just wants to embrace him, to hold him. Jesus is still recognizable, but Jesus is also different. His body is in a state of transformation. Jesus must ascend now into Risen glory. In the power of the Resurrection, Jesus sends the Holy Spirit to fill creation with the Divine Presence. In fact Jesus had declared: "'It is to your advantage that I go away, for if I do not go away, the Advocate will not come to you'" (John 16:7). The time has come for Jesus to go, to ascend to glory. Thus Mary must not "hold" him.

Jesus' words also make clear that even though he is returning to "my God and your God," he and God have always dwelt in unity. Here Jesus affirms that the same unity that he has with God is Mary's and the Apostles', too. Underlying this conversation is this key truth: Jesus is one with God, and they may be one with God and Jesus through the power of his Resurrection.

Many times in the Gospels, Jesus describes his unity, his oneness with God. For example, in John's Gospel, Jesus says: "'Believe in God, believe in me'" (14:1); "'I am in [God] and [God] is in me'" (14:11); "'In a little while the world will no longer see me, but you will see me. . . . On that day you will know that I am in [God], and you in me, and I in you'" (14:19–20); "'I am the true vine, and [God] is the vinegrower'" (15:1); and so on. His temporal mission as Jesus, the Messiah, the Suffering Servant, the Lamb of God, is done.

The Gospel accounts of Jesus' Ascension vary, but in each account the point is the same: he has Risen and is now glorified, but he will always be with us. He is one with God, and his disciples are one with him through the power of his Resurrection.

Sympathizing with Mary is quite easy though. Holding on to Jesus in the flesh has far greater reassurance than having to believe in his spirit. This has always been a temptation for those who want to believe but find it hard to do so. A man who walks and eats with us, who heals the sick right before our eyes, who raises the dead, is far easier to acknowledge as God's presence in the world than an omnipresent, dynamic, powerful, loving Spirit who ordinarily manifests God's grace through human beings like ourselves.

Jesus' telling Mary not to hold on to him is not a rejection of her love. It is a challenge for Mary to believe without touching and seeing. In the final analysis, it is the same challenge facing us. As Jesus might advise, "Listen to your heart. Stop looking for physical proof. Know that I, your savior, live and am with you. Indeed, I rose from the dead and ascended so that my spirit could live in all of creation. I have not left you an orphan, but you need to believe."

Coming to Union with All Things

In the form of meditation that I use—the *hesychast* method, or the prayer of silence—we are taught to do nothing except imagine that we are standing in the presence of God and to quietly say the Jesus Prayer. The hoped-for result is that we experience our deeper self standing in the presence of God. The prayer of silence teaches us how much we are affected by the flow of the stream of consciousness and how it breaks the way of holy silence.

Meditation, or the prayer of silence, enhances our sense of God's presence in all of life and the unity of all things in God. Sometimes a profound grace comes to the soul, and we are allowed a sense of union with God that is so complete that time ceases and we experience simple attention to God. These experiences cannot be sought, but only welcomed as a gift. This union that we occasionally experience through God's grace during meditation was probably experienced by Jesus all the time. Jesus described such union simply, "'The Father and I are one'" (John 10:30).

Meditation enlivens the senses and stirs up the mind's inner eye in such a way that one feels closer to people, other creatures, and things. People are more beautiful, flowers are more vibrant in color, and the animals around us become our friends. In the experience of *agape* love, we are in awe of the essential being of the thing-in-itself: a flower, a person, a special rock, or another thing in creation. While in the union experience, we become aware that we are not just wonderful in our separateness, but we are also awesome in our relatedness. We are intimately and deeply related. Living the resurrected life deepens our appreciation of all things in themselves, but also deepens our sense of the union of our relationship with them.

We seem to spend the first half of our life trying to establish our identity and expressing our individuality. No wonder the teenage and early adult years are so tumultuous, as we struggle to define ourselves, sometimes over and against others. Then we spend the last half of our life offering our contribution to society and preparing for a holy death, seeking reunion with all things, and ultimately with God. A truly wise person realizes that there is a healthy need for both individuation and relatedness—we are at the same time individuals and community. A holy person knows that all that we are comes from God, and all that we and creation become will one day return to God. We are essentially individuals in relation. Our ultimate relationship is with the Divine, out of whom we come, and into whom we return.

Spiritual Exercises

• Meditate on the phrase, "I am in God, and God is in me" or "Believe in God, believe in me."

• Photography is a way by which we can learn to see things in themselves. Take pictures of several subjects, focusing on a singular subject. Take a picture of a flower. Look at it carefully before you take the picture. Try to see the flower for itself. Take half a roll of pictures of many different subjects. Try photographically to isolate them from their surroundings and to see them for themselves only.

Photography is also a way that we can begin to see subjects in relation to other things. Shoot the remainder of the roll trying to see relationships between subjects. For instance, take a picture of someone holding a pet, a butterfly on a flower, or a boat sailing in the water. Try to picture the relationship that exists between these separate beings or objects.

Then study the pictures and see what you learn.

• Meditate on an icon of Jesus Christ. What do you see? Meditate on an icon of the *Theotokos*, the Virgin Mary holding the infant Jesus. Meditate on an icon of the Holy Trinity, such as the famous *Old Testament Trinity* (*c.* 1410), by Andrei Rublëv (*c.* 1370–1430). Do you see singularity, relationship, union, love, tenderness?

• Keep an account of experiences where you felt at one with the Creator or with Christ, or when you felt the spirit of God moving within you. See if there is any common connection between what makes you feel at one with God, with nature, or with other people.

• Imagine that you are reaching out to embrace Jesus at the same time as Mary. See yourself in the garden after seeing the empty tomb and being told that Christ had risen. Now you are greeting Christ gloriously risen. You are at once afraid and relieved, fearful but exultant. Just as you are extending your embrace, Jesus says, "'Do not hold on to me.'" How do you feel? Converse with him about your feelings.

• Pray repeatedly these words from the Scriptures: "'On that day you will know that I am in [God], and you in me, and I in you'" (John 14:20). Ponder each word; invite the words of Christ into your heart.

• Growth in spiritual maturity often requires letting go. Have there been times when you held on to someone and they had to tell you to let go, so that they could grow? Have you ever held on to some idea, some prejudice, some outmoded perception to the point that unless you let go of it you could not grow? Has someone else held on to you and tried to prevent you from moving beyond their old conception of you? Converse with Christ about the areas of your life where you need to let go instead of holding on.

• Sit comfortably but attentively. Close your eyes and pay attention to the physical sensations of your body. Concentrate on your feet, then your legs, torso, hands, arms, shoulders, neck, face, and finally the top of your head. Breathe deeply and slowly, inviting in the spirit of the Risen Christ.
Focus your attention on your heart. Listen to and feel it beating. Invite God to come into your heart. Imagine God in any one of God's many presences: father, mother, Christ, Holy Spirit, Creator, light, fire of love. Just be silent, open to the presence of God. Invite God's love to radiate inside you by

saying something like the following: "Come, you who are love."

When you are ready, become conscious of breathing deeply and slowly again. Offer words of thanksgiving and praise. Stretch and open your eyes.

Closing prayer. Holy and blessed Trinity, Creator, Redeemer, and Sanctifier, Unity in Diversity, and Diversity in Unity, lift us we pray into your presence where we can experience the union of divine love, and grant us the ability to embrace our connectedness with all that is above in the heavenly places and here in this earthly life. Inspire us with your love for all being. We ask this in your most glorious name. Amen.

Ascending

Meditation 10

Go, Share the Good News

The Words

"'Go therefore and make disciples of all nations, baptizing them in the name of the Father and of the Son and of the Holy Spirit, and teaching them to obey everything that I have commanded you'" (Matthew 28:19–20).

"Afterward Jesus himself sent out through them, from east to west, the sacred and imperishable proclamation of eternal salvation" (Mark 16:8).

Opening prayer. Risen Jesus, inspire us to be faithful messengers of the sacred and imperishable proclamation of eternal salvation. Amen.

Reflection

The church is a missionary society not a social club. The resurrected Christ tells us to go out into the world. We are to make disciples.

We are to teach. We are to heal. We are to carry the Gospel into the world: the Gospel of the presence of God, the Gospel of the love and mercy of God, the Good News about life. Many people still have not heard of the loving, merciful God. Still others have heard but have yet to believe. We are gently to persuade them. Many live in darkness. We are to bring the torch of the Gospel into the darkness.

In the Gospel of Mark, Jesus adds this declaration, "'Go into all the world and proclaim the good news to the whole creation'" (Mark 16:15). Francis of Assisi certainly took this passage seriously, and so he preached to the daffodils, the sparrows, and the wolves. The Gospel is about divine love, the interconnection between all things created by divine love, and the spiritual unity that should exist between us and the rest of creation. So Jesus' command to preach to people, birds, and animals becomes entirely appropriate.

Of course we have much Good News to learn from them too. Sharing the Good News is never a one-way street. One day when my wife, Sharron, and I were standing on a promontory overlooking the ocean, I climbed up on a rock and asked her, "Should I preach a sermon to the whales and fishes?" Wisely she replied, "They have more to preach to you than you to them. Maybe you should just listen!" How true.

Out in nature, Jesus worshiped, prayed, walked, and taught. Jesus was always hiking down a road to somewhere. He did occasionally teach in the synagogue, but most of the time he attended private dinners with friends or family or was out on the road. The point is this, the Good News of the Resurrection is meant for all creation. We are all God's creatures and are interconnected in this miracle that we call life.

The Resurrection of Jesus Christ is the beginning of the new creation in which the healing of all creation should take place. The lion and the lamb should learn to lie down together. Peacemakers should forge plowshares out of swords. The thirsty should be able to drink from purified streams. The homeless should be sheltered with money not wasted on missiles. In the resurrected Christ, we all become part of one another. Jesus did not die and rise just for human beings, but for the salvation and the healing of all creation.

One of the reasons I love racing sailboats so much is because of the intense interaction and harmony between creation and human ingenuity and technology. A sailboat is designed to flow through both air and water. Sailors try to trim the sails to cooperate with the wind and water and to help the boat progress toward its destination. Sailing depends on the interplay of wind flow, currents and water flow, the shape of ship and sails, and the skill and knowledge of the sailors. Ultimately, the adventure is about cooperating with all of the elements in the marine environment to either go the fastest or to reach the destination in the shortest time. This intimate union between sailors and the environment is an exciting and fascinating adventure of harmony.

As people of the Resurrection, we celebrate a marvelous harmony and unity with the whole of creation. We bless it, enjoy it, love it, and cherish it. Jesus is calling each of us to co-create God's Reign. Each of us is called to work with Christ through the power of the Holy Spirit in the divine mission that God has determined—to heal the world and all in it. The Resurrection of Jesus empowers us in this mission.

Sharing the Fruits of the Spirit

Just recently a young man walked into my office and said, "Tell me one reason why I should not take my life today." I was bowled over, and I quickly thought to myself, "What can I say to this young man to keep him from committing suicide?"

In desperation, and trying to get a little time to think, I asked him to sit down and then surprisingly found myself saying: "I can think of only one reason, namely that God loves you so much that he sent Jesus to die for you on the cross and to be raised again, to tell you just how much he loves you. God loves you unconditionally!"

With these words he broke down crying and began to tell me his life story. He remembered that at age three he saw his drunken father beat his mother until she lay on the floor with her face bloodied. His father also beat him until the family broke up and he was placed in one foster home after another.

He certainly had never known unconditional love. I tried to reassure him and reiterated that he was deeply loved by God. God cared for every hair on his head. Then his bus arrived at the stop in front of the church, and he bolted out the door.

A few days later I saw him standing at the bus stop, and I prayed for him by name. This reoccurred several times over the ensuing month. Then one day as I was returning to church, I ran into him at the bus stop and greeted him by name. He seemed surprised that I remembered him. He told me how grateful he was that I had spoken to him that day, how he had stopped drinking, had got a job, and that he even had been going to church regularly.

I was overjoyed to hear his report. But I was surprised even more at the effect that a direct testimony of the love of Christ could have on this person. It served as a startling reminder of how much the direct sharing of the love of God could affect someone if we are bold enough to offer it at the right time and if the recipient has even the slightest openness of heart.

Indeed the Good News is that God's love pervades the whole of life—our life, the life of plants, animals, creatures, and spirits seen and unseen. We are meant to recognize this love and announce it to the rest of creation. This truly is the sacred and imperishable message that we bear.

Meditation can help us nourish the message as we let God's grace transform the messenger. As we enter into union with God and experience the love that God has for us, we change. We experience the joy of living, and we see others as being loved by God. In short, as we grow into the spirit of Christ, we begin to change in such a way as to bear the fruits of the Spirit—love, joy, peace, patience, kindness, goodness, endurance. The more dramatic gifts, like holy wisdom, the power to heal, and the gift of tongues are also given to some people.

Jesus invites us to open our heart in meditation and prayer to the spirit of God, to open our mind to let God work through us, and finally to open our mouth to tell others how wonderful this God is. Ultimately, we have to trust that God not only has given us the experience and the invitation to share the message, but that God also will provide abundantly to the listeners, and that all of us will grow in the process of sharing the pearls of great price that we have had revealed to us.

Spiritual Exercises

• There are many opportunities to share the Good News of God's love, but we have to be sensitive to the situation and know when the time is right. Review the last week of your life using the following questions:
  ○ How have I been the voice of Christ's love to my family? to my friends? to coworkers? to strangers?
  ○ How have I been the hands of Christ's love to my family? to my friends? to coworkers? to people in need?
  ○ How have I been the ears of Christ's love to my family? to my friends? to coworkers? to anyone desperate or lonely?
  Pray for the grace you need to be Christ's voice, hands, and ears?

• Meditatively repeat Christ's great commission over and over, savoring its meaning and being challenged by its message, "'Go therefore and make disciples of all nations.'"

• How can you be Good News to all creation? Do an examen of consciousness about how you reverence God's earth and all the creatures who inhabit it, using the following questions:
  ○ Do I strive to live simply, using only what I need of earth's resources?
  ○ Do I seek to renew the earth by actions such as planting trees and flowers, cleaning up polluted areas, and so on?
  ○ Do I use fuels sparingly and carefully?
  ○ Do I support people who are caring for creation?
  ○ Do I enjoy the beauty of the earth and give glory to God for it?

• If you know the melody of this hymn, sing it, savoring the words. If you do not know the melody, recite aloud the hymn or chant it on one tone.

> Lest the Church neglect its mission and the Gospel go unheard,
> help us witness to your purpose with renewed integrity;
> with the Spirit's gifts empower us for the work of ministry.
>
> Lord, you bless with words assuring: "I am with you to the end."
> Faith and hope and love restoring, may we serve as you intend,
> and, amid the cares that claim us, hold in mind eternity;
> with the Spirit's gifts empower us for the work of ministry.

(The Hymnal 1982, no. 528)

Closing prayer

> Rejoice, heavenly powers! Sing, choirs of angels!
>   Exult, all creation around God's throne!
>   Jesus Christ, our King, is Risen!
>   Sound the trumpet of salvation!
>
> Rejoice, O earth, in shining splendor,
>   radiant in the brightness of your King!
>   Christ has conquered! Glory fills you!
>   Darkness vanishes for ever!

(Easter Proclamation, The Sacramentary, p. 182)

Meditation 11

Blessings of Eternal Presence

The Words

"Then he led them out as far as Bethany, and lifting up his hands, he blessed them. (Luke 24:50) 'And remember, I am with you always, to the end of the age'" (Matthew 28:20).

Opening prayer. Reassure us, Risen Jesus, with the awareness of your presence. Because we know that we can do nothing without your help, we ask you to support us in our life. In your holy name, we pray. Amen.

Reflection

In the Hebrew Scriptures and the Christian Testament, the term *blessing* is translated by two Greek words. The first word is *makarios*. It can mean everything from "blissful" to "wealthy." In classical Greek, the word is used regarding the dead to express their liberation from the vicissitudes of earthly life.

They are thus described as "happy" or "in bliss." Jesus used this word to describe the state of the believer and disciple in the Beatitudes when he said: "Blessed are the poor in spirit," and so on (Matthew 5:3–11).

The second term translated as "blessing" in the Bible is *eulogos*. Our word *eulogy* comes from this word. It could be literally translated as a "good word." A eulogy is a good word about a person who has died. A blessing from God is therefore a "good word" about some specific thing, act, or person. For example, God created the cosmos and pronounced it "good."

The Creation story is the paradigm of blessing. Throughout the story, God is creating the heavens and the earth and all of the earth's plants and creatures, including human beings. As the story progresses from stage to stage, God continually blesses each creation. So when God creates light, "God saw that the light was good" (Genesis 1:4). Each time God creates something, God declares its goodness. Then comes the final blessing, indeed the sanctification of the seventh day, and God rests from creating. "So God blessed the seventh day and hallowed it, because on it God rested from all the work . . . done in creation" (Genesis 2:3). The Artist approves and loves creation. The source of all blessing is the love and deep appreciation of the beloved by the lover.

The saga of the Hebrew people and the formation of Israel is a continuation of the story of blessing. God blesses Abraham and thereby forms the early Hebrew community by saying, "I will bless those who bless you . . . and in you all the families of the earth shall be blessed" (Genesis 12:1–3). God offers the promise of blessing to those who follow the law of Moses by saying, "[God] will love you, bless you, and multiply you" (Deuteronomy 7:13). If they live as God's people and follow the path of God, then the people of Israel will be blessed. God made this Promise in a Covenant relationship.

The resurrected Christ leaves us with a final blessing and the Promise: "'I am with you always'" (Matthew 28:20). Jesus forms a New Covenant with us. In stretching out his hands, Christ encompasses all the world. The generosity, the love, the power, and the vulnerability of God, all come to us in this gesture. At the same time, Christ promises that these blessings will always be with us: "I am with you always." Christ's fullness, goodness, and strength live with us!

At the end of the eucharistic celebration, we re-enact the resurrected Christ's final gesture to us all, "The peace of God which passeth all understanding, keep your hearts and minds in the knowledge and love of God, and of his Son Jesus Christ our Lord, and the blessing of God Almighty . . . be amongst you, and remain with you always" (*The Book of Common Prayer*, p. 339). Then we go out into the world, to love and serve the Lord with gladness and singleness of heart, rejoicing in the Power of the Holy Spirit.

We have met the living, resurrected Christ, and we need not fear. We can go out into the world proclaiming, healing, teaching, and witnessing to the presence of God, loving and blessing one another as Jesus loved and blessed us. At the same time, we can rejoice and give thanks for the marvelous victory that is ours through the gift of the resurrected Christ.

The Experience of Eternal Presence

Once while seated in the rear of the church waiting for people to come in for a service, I was quietly meditating. I suddenly became conscious that people had arrived and that I had been meditating for a long time. When I looked at my watch, I was startled to realize that only a couple of moments had passed and that I had ten minutes before the service was to begin. I began meditating again, and again I felt lifted out of time, only to discover that I had been meditating for only a moment again. This gift reminded me that these blessed moments of meditation can turn minutes into an eternity of the wonderful presence of God and give us relief from the confusion of the world as we usually experience it.

One of the experiences that meditation can bring may be described as a union with God that brings about a sense of timelessness and peace or a sense of being detached from the buzzing confusion of the world. Men and women who have been blessed with an experience of union with God may feel taken out of their body for a while followed by a feeling of intense exhilaration. Such moments are pure gifts of God. We meditate not so much to have such moments, but simply to place ourself attentively in the presence of God. Nevertheless, such moments can bring the blessing of healing.

Recently, with two other people, I prayed with a young person who desperately sought inner healing. We invited Jesus into our prayers and into her prayerful imagination. After the extended time of prayer together ended, she told us that she had experienced Jesus standing in front of her, lifting up his hands and blessing her. He had reassured her that "he was always with her" and that all would be well. I do not think the young person was even aware of the story of the final words of Jesus. Nonetheless here he was in this mysterious vision, blessing her and reassuring her. Needless to say I was astounded by her experience and how closely it paralleled the last experience of the Apostles. Again the resurrected Christ had made his presence powerfully known. He is indeed always with us.

A dedicated practice of meditation and prayer is one way of inviting ourselves into Christ's presence where he can bless us, nurture us, fill us with his breath of life, and send us into the world with the Good News of his presence. To follow the Risen Christ is to experience the eternal within the present, to be one with his spirit and with the rest of the universe. To be with Jesus in his resurrected presence is truly to live, to have eternal life.

Spiritual Exercises

• Meditate on words of the old Gospel hymn, "Blessed Assurance."

Blessed assurance, Jesus is mine!
O what a foretaste of glory divine!
Heir of salvation, purchase of God,
Born of His Spirit, washed in His blood.

Perfect submission, perfect delight,
Visions of rapture now burst on my sight;
Angels descending, bring from above
Echoes of mercy, whispers of love.

Perfect submission, all is at rest,
I in my savior am happy and blest;
Watching and waiting, looking above,
filled with His goodness, lost in His love.

(*Lift Every Voice and Sing II*, p. 184)

• Imagine Jesus standing in front of you with his hands raised up to bless you. Listen as he says, "I am with you always, to the end of the age" (Matthew 28:20). Then simply repeat his words over and over in prayer, listening to them with your heart.

• Who needs your blessing—your good words? Go to them. Like the Risen Christ, give them your blessing.

• Sing a favorite Resurrection hymn or spontaneously give thanks and praise to the loving Christ present with you now and forever.

Closing prayer. End by praying repeatedly the sacred name, "Jesus."

Blessing

Postscript

Through the words of the resurrected Christ and through the power of the Holy Spirit, we can still experience the Risen Christ today. Meditation can lead us to a direct experience of the resurrected Christ. The words of the resurrected Christ and the experience of meditating overlap and corroborate each other.

If the church would begin to refocus our attention and celebration on the Resurrection of Jesus Christ and the empowerment to live the new life that it provides, the church could again have a lively ministry of empowerment. The essential truth that Jesus imparts to us as the resurrected Christ is empowerment to live and to minister the Gospel of love to the world.

One of my favorite old-time television programs was *The Twilight Zone.* It featured stories that played with the notion of reality. Often a strange experience occurred that could only be explained by reference to a reality much larger than our normal scientific and materialistic views permitted. Visitors from another level of reality would impinge on what we took to be reality, only to "blow our minds" in the sense that our notion of reality would have to be expanded. Sometimes the visitors would bring messages from the "other side."

I suggest that something like this is what happened in the Resurrection. Jesus, who had been fully part of reality as we know it, was now transformed into an in-between messenger after the Resurrection. His post-Resurrection appearances showed that he was no longer just like us in all ways because he could immediately appear, apparently at will, and go through doors and walls in similar fashion. In his resurrected body, Jesus came back to us to deliver his most important message.

For a short time, Jesus still hovered within his disciples' ability to perceive him. An example I often give is the continuum of sound and energy. Radio waves continually go through almost every room we normally frequent, unless of course the room is shielded against such incursion. We are not aware, however, of the radio waves unless we have a tuner, a radio, by which we can tune in on the waves. The waves are there all the time.

The Risen Christ is constantly present to us, totally encompassing and infusing all of creation. Christ is never absent to us, but we are not necessarily tuned into him. We often have our tuner or radio turned off. Prayer and meditation put us in the necessary state to be open to communicating with Christ. Prayer tunes us in to the spiritual realm.

Jesus was tuned in at all times and at all levels of reality. That was why he could do the things he could do: read hearts and minds, cure ill people, know and speak the truth. He was in tune with the will of God. He was so in tune, and still is, with each of us that he came and still comes to know each of us. As we grow more in tune with Jesus through prayer and meditation, we can experience more of the resurrected life and our attitudes and behavior will show it.

Ultimately, all of life is a gift from God, and God loves each of us in a most complete and ultimate sense. May we grow more and more in love with God, others, and with all of life, until the day when we become saints in light, enjoying God and the whole cosmos most completely and serenely.

Appendix 1

Litany of the Last Words of the Resurrected Christ

You may find that praying this litany before each period of meditation focuses your attention on the story of the resurrected Christ, settles you into a mood for prayer, and lifts up your spirit. The litany may be used before meals during the Easter season or as the subject of meditation by itself. If a group prays the litany, a leader may recite the first part, with the community offering the response.

Alleluia! Christ is risen!
The Lord is risen indeed. Alleluia!
Let us pray.

As you greeted your disciples in the garden with "Hello" proclaiming your wondrous Resurrection, so may we be empowered by your life-giving presence.
Risen Christ, help us constantly to remember your risen presence. Alleluia!

As you told the women in the garden to "Fear not," so may we be courageous in the living out of the Gospel in our life.
Risen Christ, help us to fear nothing but withdrawing from your love. Alleluia!

As you blessed your disciples in the upper room by saying to them, "Peace be with you," so may we be at peace with one another and within our heart.

Risen Christ, help us to become centers of peace and peacemakers in the world around us. Alleluia!

As you said to your disciples, "Receive the Holy Spirit," so may we be empowered by your life-giving Spirit to live in the light of your Resurrection.

Risen Christ, empower us with your life-giving spirit. Alleluia!

As you said to your disciples, "Trust God, also trust in me," may we so trust in you that we cast away our worries and follow you in the way that leads to eternal life.

Risen Christ, help us to grow steadily in our trust in you. Alleluia!

As you empowered your disciples to "heal and forgive," so empower us that we may become agents of healing and reconciliation among our sisters and brothers.

Risen Christ, empower us to heal and forgive, just as you have healed and forgiven us. Alleluia!

As you said to your disciples, "Follow me," so may we be empowered to discipline ourselves to follow your example of service and humility.

Risen Christ, inspire us to follow you wherever you lead us. Alleluia!

As you said to Peter, "Feed my sheep," nurture us so that we may nurture others with the power of your love.

Risen Christ, nurture us so that we may become lovers of the whole of your creation. Alleluia!

As you said to your disciples, "I am returning to your God and my God," so may we be blessed with the gift of knowing God in this life, so that we may be one with God in eternity.

Risen Christ, lead us to God, both now in this life and in the life to come. Alleluia!

As you told your disciples, "Go into the world and preach the Good News," so encourage us to share that Good News with others that they may know the joy we have in you and you have in them and us.

Risen Christ, help us to be bold in proclaiming your glorious Resurrection. May we be apostles of your glory. Alleluia! Alleluia! Amen.

Appendix 2

The Way
of the Resurrected Christ

This celebration can be used during the whole Easter season. It can be used by the community as it is or following the evening prayer on Saturday or Sunday night. It can be read in procession around the outside of the church or perhaps standing by the stations of the cross—by way of emphasizing that the resurrected Christ has conquered sin and death. The procession could also start at the entrance to the church, move up the main aisle, around the baptismal font, the altar area, the pulpit, and the lectern. If a cross is used in the procession, I recommend a simple brass Latin cross (its emptiness symbolizing the Resurrection), a sunburst cross, or the *Christus Rex Glorioso,* or King of Glory, cross. If your congregation uses a paschal candle, it may certainly be carried to lead the procession. Easter hymns can be included as the procession moves from place to place.

Station 1

The Risen Christ Greets the Women

Leader: Alleluia! Christ is risen!

People: Christ is risen indeed! Alleluia!

Leader: We rejoice that the Risen Christ greeted Mary Magdalene and the other women with a friendly "hello." In his greeting, Christ proclaimed his living presence to them, and they fell at his feet to worship him. We give thanks for his most glorious deliverance from the grip of the grave, thereby conquering sin and death once and for all.

People: We give thanks for your victory over sin and death, and we welcome hearing your voice again. "Greetings" to you, Risen Christ. We rejoice, O Risen Christ, in your glorious Resurrection.

Station 2

The Risen Christ Tells His Disciples to "Fear Not"

Leader: Alleluia. Christ is risen!

People: Christ is risen indeed. Alleluia!

Leader: Jesus tells us, "Fear not." He has overcome the onslaught of the evil one and has defeated all the plots of those who would defy the God of Creation. Jesus tells us not to fear those who assault or insult us. Jesus, the resurrected Christ, calls us to live boldly and freely, seeking to love and do good without fear or shame. We no longer need to fear God, nor should we fear anything in all of creation.

People: We give thanks for your victory over sin and death, and we will no longer live in fear, for you have conquered all evil. We rejoice, O Risen Christ, in your glorious Resurrection!

Station 3

The Risen Christ Bids Us Peace

Leader: Alleluia. Christ is risen!

People: Christ is risen indeed. Alleluia!

Leader: The resurrected Jesus enters the upper room where his disciples hide in fear. He says to them, "'Peace be with you.'" Then he shows his hands and his side to them. Recognizing him as the Risen Christ, they are overjoyed. Again Jesus tells them, "'Peace be with you.'" Jesus brought the peace of God, which surpasses human understanding, into the room and into their heart. His Risen presence reassures them that all is well.

People: We give thanks to you for the peace that surpasses human understanding. You have brought us peace in your marvelous rising. We rejoice, O Risen Christ, in your glorious Resurrection!

Station 4

Christ Sends the Holy Spirit

Leader: Alleluia. Christ is risen!

People: Christ is risen indeed. Alleluia!

Leader: "Receive the Holy Spirit." With these words, Jesus empowers his disciples. His spirit is conveyed to them out of the source of his eternal, resurrected person. Just as God breathed the word in the beginning of Creation and all the heavens and earth, all creatures, all life came into being, so now Jesus breathes life into his disciples. They are re-created, empowered to live the resurrected life.

People: We give thanks to you for the breath of eternal life through which we are empowered to be your disciples. We rejoice, O Risen Christ, in your glorious Resurrection.

Station 5

The Risen Christ Says, "Believe"

Leader: Alleluia. Christ is risen!

People: Christ is risen indeed. Alleluia!

Leader: Jesus calls us to a deep, abiding trust. He invites us to cast away our anxieties, selfishness, narrow-mindedness, and compulsions, and to offer all of our cares to God. By conquering sin and death, Jesus has invited us to trust in life itself. Even with all its suffering, tragedies, and complexities, life can be lived with confidence in the power and love of the living God. Jesus tells us to trust in God with our whole heart, mind, soul, and body. Trust and be healed.

People: We trust your word and your love for us! We rejoice, O Risen Christ, in your glorious Resurrection!

Station 6

The Risen Christ Says, "Heal and Forgive!"

Leader: Alleluia. Christ is risen!

People: Christ is risen indeed. Alleluia!

Leader: The Risen Christ tells his disciples that signs will accompany the preaching of the Gospel. Evil spirits will be cast out, people will be healed, and forgiveness will be declared to all people. Healing of hearts, minds, and bodies should be expected as signs of God's purpose to heal, all of creation. As God has forgiven us, so we ought to forgive one another. The Risen Christ tells us to heal and forgive, and he empowers us to do so.

People: We thank you for forgiving and healing us, and for empowering us to forgive and heal one another. We rejoice, O Risen Christ, in your glorious Resurrection.

Station 7

The Risen Christ Says, "Follow Me"

Leader: Alleluia. Christ is risen!

People: Christ is risen indeed. Alleluia!

Leader: The Risen Christ invites us to follow him. He calls us into a relationship of discipleship in which we learn who he is. As disciples we study to become like our Master. We listen and learn. We put on the Lord Jesus Christ. Where our Master goes, we will follow.

People: We give thanks for your example through which you empower us to be your disciples. Grant us the grace to follow. We rejoice, O Risen Christ, in your glorious Resurrection!

Station 8

The Risen Christ Says, "Feed My Sheep"

Leader: Alleluia. Christ is risen!

People: Christ is risen indeed. Alleluia!

Leader: The Risen Christ feeds us with the words of eternal life, and we are nourished by his body and blood in the Holy Eucharist. He calls us to nourish one another with his eternal word and with the love that it engenders. Jesus told Simon Peter to feed his lambs. We are called to nourish one another with divine love.

People: We give you thanks for your eternal love that nourishes us. Help us to nourish one another with that same divine love. We rejoice, O Risen Christ, in your glorious Resurrection!

Station 9

The Risen Christ Says, "I Am Returning to Your God and My God"

Leader: Alleluia. Christ is risen!

People: Christ is risen indeed. Alleluia!

Leader: Jesus announces to his followers that he is returning to God. He has fulfilled his mission on earth. Under the guidance of the Holy Spirit, the community of believers will spread the word of God and carry on Christ's mission. So Christ goes before us to prepare a place for us. We, too, will rest in God. God is our eternal home toward which we journey. Christ's Ascension prefigures our ascension to the embrace of God. We are now assured of our resting place with God.

People: We thank you for this blessed assurance that your return to God signals our return some day. Be our strength. Grant us the same quiet confidence that you possessed. We rejoice, O Risen Christ, in your glorious Resurrection.

Station 10

The Risen Christ Says, "Go into All the World"

Leader: Alleluia. Christ is risen!

People: Christ is risen indeed. Alleluia!

Leader: The circle is now complete. Christ sends us out in apostolic mission. Jesus came that we might be healed and set free. Now we are called to become healers and liberators of those who have not yet heard the Good News that God loves us and nothing can separate us from that love. We now share in Christ's mission. We are to go and tell others what we have heard and seen. The redemption of all creation has been made manifest. The Word is sure, our mission clear. Let us go forth in the power of the Holy Spirit.

People: By your glorious Resurrection, we are healed and set free. You empower us to forgive and to love. We can proclaim the Good News to all creation. Alleluia! We rejoice, O Risen Christ, in your glorious Resurrection.

Leader: Alleluia. Christ is risen!
People: Christ is risen indeed. Alleluia!

Leader: Let us go forth in the name of Christ.
People: Thanks be to God. Alleluia! Alleluia! Alleluia! Amen.

Acknowledgments *(continued)*

The scriptural quotations in this book are from the New Revised Standard Version of the Bible. Copyright © 1989 by the Division of Christian Education of the National Council of the Churches of Christ in the United States of America. Used with permission. All rights reserved.

The quotations on pages 19–20, 32 and 76, and 43 are from *The Book of Common Prayer* (New York: Seabury Press, 1977), pages 118, 339, and 832. Copyright © 1977 by Charles Mortimer Guilbert as custodian of the Standard Book of Common Prayer. All rights reserved.

The quotations on pages 37, 38, and 73 are from *The Hymnal 1982 According to the Use of the Episcopal Church* (New York: Church Hymnal Corporation, 1985), numbers 503, 509, and 528. Copyright © 1985 by the Church Pension Fund. All rights reserved.

The quotation on page 40 is from *New Seeds of Contemplation*, by Thomas Merton (New York: New Directions Books, 1962), page 128. Copyright © 1961 by the Abbey of Gethsemani.

The Easter Proclamation on page 73 is from *The Sacramentary* (New York: Catholic Book Publishing Company, 1985), page 182. Copyright © 1985–1974 by Catholic Book Publishing Company.

The hymn "Blessed Assurance" on pages 77–78 is from *Lift Every Voice and Sing II* (New York: Church Hymnal Corporation, 1981), page 184.